Muthuraj Swamy was
Edinburgh for his d
Interreligious Dialogue.   Director of the Cambridge
Centre for Christianity Worldwide, and Project Manager for
Theological Education for Mission in the Anglican Communion,
London. A theologian from the Church of South India, he has served
as a theological educator in India for many years and was previously
the Dean of Faculty of Theology in the Union Biblical Seminary, Pune,
where he taught in the fields of religion and theology. He has also
worked with interreligious organizations in India for several years,
promoting conflict resolution and peace-building programmes. He is
a Visiting Fellow at St John's College, Durham University.

Dr Swamy is the author of *The Problem with Interreligious Dialogue:
Plurality, Conflict and Elitism in Hindu-Christian-Muslim Relations*
(Bloomsbury, 2016). He is the co-editor of three forthcoming volumes
to facilitate preparation for the Lambeth Conference 2020, based on
the Archbishop of Canterbury's three priorities: *Walking Together*
(Reconciliation), *Witnessing Together* (Evangelism and Witness)
and *Listening Together* (Prayer), to be published by the Anglican
Communion Office, London.

RECONCILIATION

MUTHURAJ SWAMY

THE ARCHBISHOP OF
CANTERBURY'S LENT BOOK 2019

First published in Great Britain in 2018

Society for Promoting Christian Knowledge
36 Causton Street
London SW1P 4ST
www.spck.org.uk

British Library Cataloguing-in-Publication Data
A catalogue record for this book is available from the British Library

ISBN 978–0–281–08008–3
eBook ISBN 978–0–281–08009–0

Typeset by The Book Guild Ltd, Kibworth, Leicester
First printed in Great Britain by Ashford Colour Press
Subsequently digitally printed in Great Britain

eBook by The Book Guild Ltd, Kibworth, Leicester

Produced on paper from sustainable forests

To
Mahiba, Mona and Mano
who teach me every day the importance
and the joy of reconciliation

Contents

Contents

Foreword

Reconciliation is the Gospel. It is at the very heart of the entire story of God and his people. The story we know so well starts in the garden of Eden. When everything goes wrong, relationships break down. Relationships between human beings, between human beings and God, between human beings and the world they inhabit, between human beings and their very selves – all are caught up in the destruction brought through sin. This fracture runs through the heart of humanity and manifests itself in broken communities, broken friendships, broken families and a broken world.

Yet there is good news. There is good news because from the first stirrings of dissent, God has been working ceaselessly to mend, to heal and to reconcile. The whole story of God, throughout Scripture, is one of reconciliation, of bringing people, families and even nations back together and back to God. It is not an easy story. It is not sugar-coated or romantic. Reconciliation is hard work: it is long-winded, often puzzling and never risk-free. It always walks hand-in-hand with truth, justice and sacrifice. The God we meet in the person of Jesus, though, takes all of this on. He does not make pronouncements from above; he does not work in the abstract. He comes to earth and walks with us. He becomes everything it means to be human and transforms our brokenness from within. He reaches out to those who are excluded or abandoned. He crosses boundaries that divide genders, generations, races and communities. He speaks difficult words, and he speaks healing words. Ultimately, on the cross, he pays the price for challenging and transforming the brokenness of human life and, through his death, we receive the invitation to a liberated life.

Both the cost and joy of reconciliation are reflected in this book. Muthuraj Swamy takes us on a journey through Scripture and illuminates difficult stories of conflict, beautiful stories of reconciliation, incomplete stories of steps towards reconciliation. Swamy is realistic, and he pulls no punches, yet he casts before us a vision of God's call to us to join in with God's work. He challenges us to examine ourselves and the world around us at the end of each reflection. Swamy weaves in the depth of his own cultural background in India in ways that cast new light and beg new thoughts on many of the texts that he explores. He reminds us constantly that true reconciliation is a journey into otherness: into the otherness of God and the otherness of our neighbours – both those who are near, and those who are far away. With every story, the beauty of reconciliation shines through as the light we need to follow.

This book offers you an invitation this Easter. It invites you to come alongside God on this journey. It invites you to be swept up again into the vision of God's all-encompassing work of reconciliation. It invites you, starting with yourself, to share in the vision and work for the reconciliation of all things and all people.

+ + *Justin Cantuar*
Lambeth Palace, London

Preface

I am deeply humbled to have been invited to write the Archbishop of Canterbury's Lent Book for 2019 on the theme of reconciliation. Reconciliation is one of the three priorities of Archbishop Justin Welby's ministry, the other two being prayer and the renewal of the religious life, and evangelism and witness. Reconciliation – both with God and with our fellow human beings – is a hugely important need given the increasing conflicts and divisions we witness among us. Contrary to expectation, advances in various aspects of life have not halted the spread of hate and violence in our world, and many feel contempt for those who are different from themselves. In such a context, mending broken relationships and building new relationships with others are essential for our life together, as human beings and as Christians. Justin Welby reflects on the importance of being called to reconciliation thus:

> Reconciliation is one of our greatest needs and toughest challenges as human beings. In a world plagued by conflict, division and indifference, the Church has a crucial role to play as a community of reconcilers. Jesus calls every one of us to love God, our neighbours, ourselves and our enemies – a challenging command, with nobody left out . . .

> The life, death and resurrection of Jesus are the story of God's reconciliation with humanity. Through them, Jesus opens the way for a restored relationship between God and us. If we embrace that joyful new relationship, it should overflow into the way we relate to one another. This will look different in each of our lives – from making cups of tea to acting as professional mediators.

> Christ calls us to be peacemakers who cross the borders and barriers that divide us – radical in our generosity and welcome. It's a call to see others in their full humanity, to persist in seeking their good. Communities of followers of Jesus across the world are present at the most local levels where relationships are made or broken. In these relationships, the Church has the opportunity to offer honest, deeply-rooted hope.[1]

---

1   https://www.archbishopofcanterbury.org/message-reconciliation-archbishop-justin-welby

Hence the ministry of reconciliation that the Church has received from Jesus Christ is the Church's 'opportunity to offer honest, deeply-rooted hope' in the context of the violence, conflict and division we are experiencing. This opportunity has been made possible by the Cross of Christ: the Cross was the consequence of Christ speaking, acting and living as he did in order to reconcile us with God and with one another; the Cross makes possible a new life of community in Christ – a community of forgiveness, openness, peace and justice, in which we care for the other. Connecting forgiveness and reconciliation to the Cross, Pope Francis says:

> How I wish that all men and women of good will would look to the Cross if only for a moment! . . . In the silence of the Cross, the uproar of weapons ceases and the language of reconciliation, forgiveness, dialogue, and peace is spoken . . . Let everyone be moved to look into the depths of his or her conscience and listen to that word which says: Leave behind the self-interest that hardens your heart, overcome the indifference that makes your heart insensitive towards others, conquer your deadly reasoning, and open yourself to dialogue and reconciliation. Look upon your brother's sorrow . . . stay your hand and do not add to it, rebuild the harmony that has been shattered; and all this achieved not by conflict but by encounter![2]

The foundation of Christian reconciliation lies in the Trinity – God the Father, God the Son and God the Holy Spirit. The members of the Trinity not only relate to one another, they show us how to cross boundaries and be open to those whom we perceive as different. They are involved in reconciling sinners with God, as well as reconciling broken communities with one another. Healthy relationships between God and human beings, and between human beings themselves, are the root of Christian life and faith.

Firmly based on God's work in reconciling us, the 40 Bible studies in this book reflect primarily on two aspects of the Christian ministry of reconciliation: the first concerns our personal experience of broken or non-existent relationships; the second to situations where we find ourselves, as Jesus did, working to reconcile others, who may be struggling to open up to one another and build relationships.

In the first scenario, it is important that we reflect on possible

---

2   http://w2.vatican.va/content/francesco/en/homilies/2013/documents/
     papa-francesco_20130907_veglia-pace.html

impediments to reconciliation – perhaps a lack of humility or self-criticism or openness to the other – in order to restore what has been damaged. The Bible has many examples of how the people of God reacted in similar situations – positively, which led to the building of relationships, or negatively, which led to further brokenness.

In the second scenario, it is our responsibility to do what we can to work to reconcile hostile communities, even if this involves risking or sacrificing our life or resources as we speak for the vulnerable. Jesus has shown us how to do this.

In both scenarios, it is important that reconciliation is founded on justice.

I would like to thank Archbishop Justin Welby sincerely for the opportunity to reflect on reconciliation for this Lent book. I am grateful to Bishop Graham Kings and Isabelle Hamley for their encouragement and support in the process. My heartfelt thanks go to Sam Richardson, CEO of SPCK, for our initial discussions of the book and for extending help in many ways. Alison Barr, Publisher at SPCK, has been tremendously supportive and understanding (especially with the delays involved, as I worked on the manuscript in the midst of moving with my family from India and then settling into a new job in Cambridge), and she has greatly helped in shaping the book. My sincere thanks also to the Archbishop of Canterbury's Reconciliation Ministry team, particularly to Sarah Snyder and Victoria Mason, for their very helpful comments on the manuscript, and to Professor David Ford, Emeritus Regius Professor of Divinity, University of Cambridge, for his kind words of commendation. Thank you to all my friends and colleagues who have encouraged me in one way or another, especially Ian McCafferty, Roger Bowen, Stephen Spencer, Jayakiran Sebastian, Israel David, Asish Koshy, David Muthukumar, John Joshvaraja, Matthew Chandrankunnel, Ben Wilkinson, Israel Selvanayagam, Alan Palanna, Simon Lewis, Terry Barringer, Michael Beckett and my immediate and wider family.

How to use this book

Reconciliation offers 40 Bible studies, one for each of the 40 days of Lent. To help those who wish to use the book in weekly gatherings, the studies have been arranged in six chapters (with an additional introductory first chapter), based on the following themes: (1) the foundations of reconciliation, (2) impediments to reconciliation, (3) risking the self to reconcile those in conflict, (4) the need for humility and self-criticism when involved in reconciling or being reconciled, (5) the call to radical openness, and (6) peace with justice. There are five studies for the first week (Chapter 2) and seven studies each for the remaining weeks (Chapters 3–7).

Through the questions provided, readers are invited to reflect further on the theme of each study – in their specific context, and in situations in which relationships and reconciliation with others are involved.

1

The ministry of reconciliation

1 The context today: conflicts and reconciliation

The film *Jesus* (1999) differs from other films on the life of Jesus Christ in that it opens with scenes of conflict and violence that appear to Jesus in a dream, some time before he begins his ministry. In his final hours in the Garden of Gethsemane, the film makers have Jesus revisit these scenes. Satan emerges and as part of his plan to dissuade Jesus from going to the cross to give his life for humanity, shows Jesus that this will not prevent further animosity. People are not going to change, Satan says. Your death will be in vain. You will only add one more reason – yourself – to the many causes people already have to hate and kill one another. You can solve division among people through God's power, Satan continues; but Jesus refuses to use his power. He will go to the cross and die for the sake of humanity. He tells Satan that God has created human beings with free will and those who want to love others will find strength in him to love even more.

Although this film makes use of some extra-biblical narratives, its portrayal of Jesus, his life and his ministry in the context of conflict and division – in which love and reconciliation between humanity and God are needed – is strikingly faithful to what we read in the Bible. Rooting ourselves in the love of God, manifested in the life of Christ, we are to exercise radical openness to one another in order to build relationships. Sadly, over the last many centuries, Jesus Christ has often been made a reason for division and conflict – among Christians and between them and people of different walks of life. Yet to those committed to love and serve others, to mend broken relationships and build bridges in society and unite humanity, Jesus, revealing God's love, inspires us, motivates us and gives us strength. He has bequeathed us the gift and ministry of reconciliation and has taught us, through his life, work and death, how to participate in it.

Today, more than ever, the world needs to work to build and strengthen relationships among individuals and communities. We are said to be living in a global society that is progressing and advancing in science and technology, education, social, economic and cultural life. Especially significant are the rapid growth in information and communication technology during the last few decades, and the sophisticated nature of (some) international migration. One of the anticipated results of these advancements is that people from different backgrounds and walks of life are being drawn together in terms of proximity and interdependence and we might expect that this would result in better relationships between them. Unfortunately, this is not the reality.

Diversity is a key feature of global and multicultural existence. Yet in the world today, one can often see attitudes that are critical of embracing diversity and difference. In the twenty-first century, global migration, both voluntary and forced (due to poverty, ethnic conflict and war), has brought challenges. Many people, particularly in Western society, have been unwelcoming towards those whose cultures, traditions and religions are different from their own. Such an attitude is detrimental to the growth of healthy community relations.

Further, there is an increasing realization that violence, hate and conflict cannot always be blamed on those wielding political or elite power. Most of the genocides in the past also have an ordinary face, hence understanding the role of ordinary people in conflict and violence has become an important topic for research, study and reflection in recent times. One might also mention that Christians, in addition to having divisions among ourselves, sometimes take sides with the dominant and destructive forces that exercise hate and violence against poor, marginalized and vulnerable people.

This may seem to offer a picture of the world as bleak as the one Satan shows to Jesus in the film mentioned earlier. However, there are a number of people, groups and communities – alongside government and non-government institutions – who are making genuine efforts to encourage the growth of a peaceful and harmonious society. They are committed to developing relationships between communities, opening up to the other, embracing difference, respecting diversity, crossing boundaries to build bridges and healing wounds through reconciliation activities.

Christians (and other religious, atheist and secular traditions) have important resources to offer in this regard. The Bible, worship, liturgy and prayer all help us in our work for reconciliation. The very basic Christian world view of love and peace with God and with one another, based on what God has done for humanity through Jesus Christ, is where we begin our ministry of reconciliation. We may be encouraged that the Church, despite its shortcomings at various stages in history, has always endeavoured to relate with different cultures, reconcile warring communities and connect people with one another.

2 The ministry of reconciliation

St Paul, writing to the churches in Corinth and Colossae, articulates clearly that the basis of the Christian ministry of reconciliation is the fact that God has reconciled the world through Jesus Christ:

> So if anyone is in Christ, there is a new creation: everything old has passed away; see, everything has become new! All this is from God, who reconciled us to himself through Christ, and has given us the ministry of reconciliation; that is, in Christ God was reconciling the world to himself, not counting their trespasses against them, and entrusting the message of reconciliation to us. So we are ambassadors for Christ, since God is making his appeal through us; we entreat you on behalf of Christ, be reconciled to God.   (2 Corinthians 5.17–20)

> For in him all the fullness of God was pleased to dwell, and through him God was pleased to reconcile to himself all things, whether on earth or in heaven, by making peace through the blood of his cross. And you who were once estranged and hostile in mind, doing evil deeds, he has now reconciled in his fleshly body through death, so as to present you holy and blameless and irreproachable before him.
> (Colossians 1.19–22)

Both of these passages express at least three essential facts about reconciliation for and by Christians. First, they state unambiguously that the foundation of our very existence as Christians is our belief that God has reconciled us, in spite of our inclination to alienate ourselves from God, through Jesus Christ. Second, that through this we are invited to reconcile with one another: 'God reconciling all things' implies the process of reconciliation *among* all things as well. Third, that for a Christian, being involved in reconciliation activity in the world is not a choice, but rather a responsibility and a vocation: Paul clearly speaks of 'the ministry of reconciliation'.

While Paul writes about the importance of reconciliation to

3

churches struggling with internal conflict, in the gospels we see the ministry of Jesus Christ in reconciling sinners with God and with one another. In preparing the ground for mending relationships, Jesus quite often defies established boundaries and invites his followers to demonstrate radical openness. He brings people of different cultures and orientations closer to one another – his ways of disciple-making being a great example (see study 3). Jesus chastises the dominant, challenging them to be open to the marginalized and disadvantaged, which is essential if just relationships in human society are to flourish. He invites those who have broken relationships with their neighbours to reconcile with them first, before reconciling with God (Matthew 5.24; 18.23–35).

Similarly, in the Old Testament, we see how God is continually involved in the world, inviting people into a proper relationship with God. From the beginning, it is God's openness and initiative to relate with the world that remains the foundation for all acts of reconciliation. God's continuous involvement in the world and relationship with human beings shows us that reconciliation is not a one-time act, but a process, both because of the sinful nature of humanity and (wonderfully) because our God is a compassionate God who is waiting for us (Isaiah 30.18), in spite of the repeated acts that impair our relationship with God. The Hebrew term for reconciliation, *kaphar,* is translated into English as 'atonement', literally meaning a state without tension. What God wants is a relationship without tension – both between God and human beings and among human beings. There is always a justice angle to reconciliation with God and this is clearly expressed by many of the Old Testament prophets, who have proclaimed that to be reconciled with God is to act justly towards our fellow human beings.

God's continuous involvement in the world, as recorded in the Bible, shows that reconciliation and relationships are of fundamental importance, and that we are to continue the ministry that has been entrusted upon us by our Lord through his disciples and the apostles. Such a ministry of reconciliation involves at least the following five aspects:

1 God's reconciliation: faith in God reconciling human beings directly or through God's prophets and leaders, and finally through Jesus Christ, is foundational to our reconciliation ministry.

2 Our reconciliation with God: while God is compassionate and open, it is up to us to turn towards God and live in a good relationship with God and with our fellow human beings, if we are to experience life in all its fullness.

3 Our reconciliation with others: our reconciliation with God is complete only when we have the courage and humility to be in proper and just relationships with our neighbours.

4 Our reconciliation with ourselves: we need to learn to relate to our own selves, to nurture 'peace within'. Our relationship with ourselves affects our relationships with God and others.

5 Our efforts to reconcile our fellow human beings with God and to promote reconciliation among our neighbours: following the model of the life and work of our Lord, we are invited to spend ourselves in this way, which is central to the mission of God. Our reconciliation ministry will be incomplete otherwise.

The first of the above is a reality and the foundation of our ministry of reconciliation; the other four aspects are our responsibilities as Christians. The ministry of reconciliation is important in the context of the issues facing Christians within Christian communities, as well as in the context of wider conflicts and wars between communities, ideologies and nations. We are not only called to be reconciled, but also to reconcile, even if it involves submitting our will, or our very life, as Jesus has done.

The possibility of living together in peace and co-existence is strong. While conflicts do happen among people and strained relationships (in which we too are involved) affect the world, our Christian tradition offers plenty of resources to enable us to work towards reconciliation. The Bible studies that follow aim to help us in this goal. First, let me say a few words about how I employ the idea and practice of reconciliation in the reflections in this book.

3 Reconciliation for broken relationships and lack of relationships

The Christian ministry of reconciliation works not only for reconciliation when a conflict or disagreement occurs or after it has occurred; it considers reconciliation as relationship-building that influences all aspects of our everyday life. Unfortunately, reconciliation (with God and with our fellow human beings) is sometimes thought of as time- and space-bound, as if conflict resolution can only occur after a conflict between people who were once friends or in a good relationship. In reality, reconciliation is greater than that: it is a long process of building relationships.

Reconciliation is both a particular and a specific act or event and a process in life. As a specific act, the emphasis is on the 're' in reconciliation, the 'again' or 'back'. In this sense, reconciliation means bringing broken relationships back to their normal condition. As such it is conflict resolution, when individuals or groups who once were in close proximity and a good relationship are reconnected after a dispute, argument, disagreement or crisis. Efforts to solve conflicts and divisions between friends or within families, and bringing together divided churches and conflicting communities, are examples of reconciliation as a specific act. We often tend to understand reconciliation *only* in this sense.

However, more broadly, reconciliation is part of the whole of our Christian life. We are to live reconciliation every minute, in continuous relationship with God and with one another, and grow in such relationships. It is not simply that we may have had an argument or disagreement and need to resolve things. It is beyond that. In other words, reconciliation as it should be lived and practised in Christian life is to do not only with broken relationships, but also with *a lack of relationship*. In this sense, it involves openness to the other, overcoming prejudice and bias, identifying factors that contribute to hate and violence, working to overcome such devastating forces, and crossing bridges again and again. It is creating an atmosphere of peace with justice where we are committed to preventing conflicts, divisions, hate and violence.

When reconciliation is to do with a lack of relationship, it concerns how we react to someone who is different from us, and how we embrace that difference in order to build a relationship. In this sense, reconciliation is God's continuous involvement in the world, and God's plan for proper relationships between God and the world and among human beings *in the context of diversity and difference*. Diversity and difference are gifts from God and we are invited to use these in the building of relationships, which will involve efforts of creating, constructing, maintaining, preserving and envisioning. To be reconciled is to be radically open to the other, and this can help us avoid conflict, stay together when we disagree with one another and find solutions to avoid repeating mistakes.

This approach is important because we have to deal today not only with broken relationships between those who were once friends, but also with the systemic brokenness of relationships among wider communities. We live in an environment where people are not prepared to relate to those who are different. Indeed, it is as difficult to relate to different cultures and different people as it is to rebuild broken relationships with those whom we already know. So we live behind closed doors, constructing walls to keep others out, nurturing our aversion to difference and diversity. We let inequality and injustice hugely affect our prospects of peace and reconciliation with one another. An additional difficulty is the struggle between groups to claim victimhood in contexts where reconciliation efforts are made. There are real victims in every conflict, but victimhood is misused by powerful people against powerless ones, powerful nations against poor nations, dominant groups against subordinates, citizens against immigrants and refugees. Furthermore, a victim in the past can become an oppressor in the present; a victim in one context and an oppressor in another at the same time. This poses a number of challenges to reconciliation efforts.

We have seen that reconciliation is not simply a specific event. It involves not only resolution, but also prevention. It is a process. It is an attitude. It is a climate. It is embracing differences. It is commitment to diversity. Throughout this book I use reconciliation in its wider sense: building and strengthening relationships with radical openness to the other.

2

God has reconciled with us – the foundations of reconciliation

Reconciliation begins with God, because it is God who has initiated – and continues in – relationship with the world. What we do when we turn to reconcile with God, or with others as part of the Christian ministry of reconciliation, is simply to respond to God's initiative. The greatest commandment(s) Christ has given us, 'You shall love the Lord your God with all your heart, and with all your soul, and with all your mind' and 'You shall love your neighbour as yourself' (Matthew 22.37–39), is in essence about relationship – between you, your God and your neighbour.

The work of the Triune God, in addition to the relationship within the Trinity, involves continuous acts of reconciliation in the world.

God in the Old Testament, though not directly revealing Godself to people, cares a great deal for relationships with and among humanity. In fact, the very act of creation by God in the beginning, long before the fall in Genesis 3, is an affirmation and manifestation of God's relationship with the world and provides the basis for reconciliation to take place after the fall and later through Jesus Christ. God in the Old Testament is the one who continues to make covenants with God's people so that they would remain in, and when they go astray, return to, relationship.

It is the reconciling act of Jesus Christ that brings salvation for the whole of humanity. He is the Word of God who has broken the boundaries to become flesh (John 1.14). He relates with the world as Emmanuel, 'God with us' (Matthew 1.23). His radical openness to the other becomes evident in his becoming vulnerable, in spite of his exalted position, in order to identify with and save the weak and disadvantaged (Philippians 2.6–8). He continues his reconciliation ministry by being the mediator between God and us (Hebrews 8.6, 9.15, 12.24; 1 Timothy 2.5).

The Holy Spirit is not bound by space and time and freely connects believers (Acts 2). When Jesus' disciples were empowered by the Holy Spirit after Jesus ascended to heaven, they were able to break the boundaries between Judea and Samaria, and between Jerusalem and the ends of the earth, through God's mission of reconciliation (Acts 1.8).

The Church is the gift of God and a visible mark of (a) God's relationship to the world, (b) Jesus' ministry of reconciliation, and (c) the Holy Spirit's bringing together of God's people in fellowship. The Church today is entrusted with the responsibility of carrying on the ministry of reconciliation within itself and with and in the wider society in which it exists.

1 Relationships and reconciliation: the heart of Christian life

Key text: Matthew 22.34–40
The Greatest Commandment

A significant aspect of many religious traditions is their concern with fundamental questions affecting human beings. For instance, some branches of Hinduism focus on matters such as 'who am I?'; 'from where was I born?', 'where will I go when I die?' and 'will I have another birth?' Similar questions are contemplated in the Christian tradition and many others. Yet if there is one question central to the Christian worldview, it is something like 'who am I in relation to God and who am I in relation to my neighbour?' In the Christian life, the question 'who' (or 'what') am I?' is not meaningful on its own.

As Christians, we undertake the ministry of reconciliation because we believe in God's relationship with the world and God's desire for proper relationships among human beings. Christianity is about relationships; without them, it would cease to exist. As a very young convert to Christianity, I often asked myself as I was growing up: 'what is special about Christianity?' Theologically this question is concerned with the uniqueness of Christianity, and doctrinally this relates, among other things, to the uniqueness of Christ, the doctrine of the Trinity, the incarnation and the resurrection, all of which are crucial to the Christian life.

Growing as a Christian, I learned that the uniqueness of Christianity is rooted in the idea and practice of relationship – between God, me and my neighbour. The Greatest Commandment articulates this very clearly, and I very often return to it. Particularly significant are the words of Jesus in this context: 'On these two commandments hang all the law and the prophets.' *There is literally nothing else required for the Christian life.* Here is a triangular relationship – a human being, his/her God and his/her neighbour. This is beautifully explained by our Lord in Matthew 22.35–40, as we shall now explore.

In the text, a Pharisee comes and asks Jesus: 'Teacher, which commandment in the Law is the greatest?' Jesus answers: 'You shall love your God with all your heart, and with all your soul, and with all your mind. This is the greatest and first commandment. And a second one is like it: You shall love your neighbour as yourself. On these two commandments hang all the law and the prophets.' The message of this text is generally known as a double love commandment.

The encounter between Jesus and the Pharisee is located within the context of Jesus' continuous conflicts with the Jewish leaders in Matthew 22. It follows on from confrontations about paying tax to Caesar, and the question of marriage in resurrection posed by some Sadducees. This latest skirmish seems rather mild. As there are said to be 613 precepts to be found in the Torah, it might be a genuine problem for the Pharisee to decide which is the most important commandment. He might be using an innocent and common question to test Jesus.

I think we should regard this text as being on relationship as much as on love, given that love is expressed through action rather than in the simple affirmation of loving someone or something. The commandment 'you shall love' requires more than an emotional response. Love for one's neighbour means acting in a way that keeps their good and well-being firmly in mind. Love is always demonstrated in practical activity.

The greatest commandment, Jesus says, is first of all about loving God. His answer to the Pharisee reflects traditional teaching as he quotes from Deuteronomy 6.5, the commandment God gave to the Israelites through Moses centuries ago: 'You shall love the LORD your God with all your heart, and with all your soul, and with all your might.' Indeed, this commandment was recited by the Jews at least twice a day as part of their religious life.

What do we mean when we speak of loving or relating to God? Anything known and visible we connect with through our senses, but we have not seen God, who is above all sensual perception. For me, loving God and relating to God means acknowledging God's identity as our creator and sustainer, and reflecting on that reality in the ordering of our everyday living. It means realizing our own weakness, limitations and failures as human beings, our lack of ability to do everything on our own and by ourselves. To put it simply, relating to God means having a humble attitude with regard to our destiny. It is committing to a life of action according to God's will, revealed to us in the life and teaching of Jesus Christ. The Bible demonstrates clearly that loving or relating to God primarily means *humbling* oneself before God.

The European Enlightenment encouraged human beings to imagine a new world of scientific and technological development, discovery and progress. Human confidence and scientific progress have benefitted us to a great extent, but they have also given rise to various situations in which a human being has come to consider that he alone could determine the good of the world (gender is important here: the Enlightenment was always about men, as if women did not exist at all). Yet colonialism, two world wars, several major and minor genocides and conflicts – based on ethnic and geographic identity, religion, caste, race and gender – have all taken place since the Enlightenment. It appears that human beings may not be capable of doing everything themselves after all. By affirming human dominance, we may have mastered the art of accumulating and maintaining power over others and over the world, but only at great cost. In such a context, relating to God requires us truly to realize and acknowledge the place of God in all aspects of our life and relationships.

Second, this encounter between Jesus and the Pharisee raises the issue of relating to one's own self, although this is seldom made clear. So, before looking at relating to 'your neighbour', we need to know the significance of 'you' in this text. We do know that 'you' is important (it is used here eight times), because without 'you' we can't talk about 'your God' or 'your neighbour'. It simply implies one's relationship to one's self. The expression 'all your heart, all your soul and all your mind' could well relate to this as much as to the idea of wholeness.

Taking care of or being mindful of one's own self is fully biblical, and we see a lot about it in the instructions given to churches on self-control, self-understanding, self-awareness and self-reflection in the New Testament epistles. In Matthew 22, it is implied that Jesus does not speak against loving oneself or relating to oneself; rather, learning to know who we are individually and keeping our selves well is essential for relationship with others. This means that one's relationship with oneself is equally important in the process of relating to God and to one's neighbour.

Of course this can be and has been construed as promoting selfishness. Neo-capitalist ideology would interpret it as 'first love yourself in order to love the other' or 'accumulate everything first in order to share it with others later.' But history and experience have demonstrated that such action tends to lead to wealth accruing in the hands of a powerful few. It will also be apparent that relating to one's own self should not mean cutting off relationships with others and becoming excessively introvert.

Finally, the greatest commandment is about loving your neighbour, which means relating to your neighbour. We don't see this clause in the words of Moses when he gives God's commandment to the Israelites, but the importance of loving one's neighbour is directly or indirectly part of God's many commandments in the Old Testament. Jesus here articulates this. In keeping with the nature of his ministry, he adds it to a commandment with which the Pharisee is already familiar. It is interesting that Jesus does not here explain who one's neighbour is (unlike when he responds to another questioner with The Good Samaritan parable in Luke 10.25–37, although even there he does not clearly define a neighbour).

By not defining one's neighbour, Jesus challenges our tendency to relate only to those who are like ourselves. A neighbour can be someone who lives near or far away, who may be familiar or a stranger. It generally suggests a friend, but could also mean an enemy, given that Jesus' understanding of neighbour encompasses praying for one's enemies. Loving our neighbour as ourselves may be summed up as meaning that we treat others with the same respect, kindness and consideration that we would like to be shown (Luke 6.31).

While these three forms of relationship – loving God, self and neighbour – are essential for Christians today, it is interesting that Jesus puts them *together* in his response to the Pharisee. The triangular, interdependent relationship involving you, your God and your neighbour, or us, our God and our neighbours, is crucial to any community that intends to participate in the ministry of reconciliation in a hostile world. Jesus presents us with a model of how to relate with one another, challenging the many rigid community identities and boundaries we may (possibly subconsciously) have in place.

In this interdependent triangular relationship, one presupposes the other two. One depends upon the other two. One leads towards the other two. How we humble ourselves before God has a lot to do with how we approach the good and welfare of our neighbours. These things are not unconnected. Failure in one relationship can lead to a failure in the other.

The story of Cain in the Old Testament is one of the best examples of this interconnection. As we read in Genesis 4.5, when God did not accept Cain's offering, his countenance fell. Cain failed to relate properly to his self and this failure led to the killing of his brother (obviously his immediate neighbour), and this led to the breaking of Cain's relationship with God.

The Pharisee asked for the greatest commandment. Jesus gave an interrelated two, involving three aspects of relationship. As we are discovering, this model for relationships and identity formation is dynamic, vibrant and liberating!

To clarify, the human community Jesus envisioned is founded upon us, our neighbours and our God, as the Greatest Commandment shows. It is foundational to our Christian existence. In our increasingly hostile world, this triangular, interdependent relationship challenges us as Christians to go beyond the static boundaries conventionally and conveniently available to us, to participate in the ministry of reconciliation initiated by Christ.

Questions for reflection

1 Can you think of a situation when a relationship issue with God, with yourself or with a neighbour has had a negative impact on one of these other relationships?
2 How can you affirm the importance of 'you' in the Greatest Commandment without acting as a 'selfish you'?
3 Reflect on Jesus' words: 'On these two commandments hang all the law and the prophets.'

2 God, the creator of relationships

Key text: Genesis 1–2

In the Garden of Eden, Adam and Eve sin by disobeying God. This leads to a broken relationship with God, through which all humanity is put under a curse. Jesus, the new Adam, sets right the relationship damaged in Eden, reconciling sinful humanity to God by sacrificing his own life on the cross.

This tends to be the basis of our understanding of reconciliation in Christianity. Yet thinking that God's plan for reconciling the world with God begins strictly with the Eden affair is quite limiting. As we have seen, reconciliation in its wider sense is about relationships – not only mending broken relationships, but also creating new relationships where there are none at all.

To deepen our understanding of the ministry of reconciliation, we need to look at events that took place even before the fall. We realize that God reconciling the world is founded on an everlasting longing for creation to be in continuous relationship with God who is among us. In other words, God creating the world and everything in it is, first, a matter of relationship.

The very first action mentioned in the Bible is God's act of creation. Creation involves more than simply producing things. God not only creates things and human beings; *God creates and initiates relationships.* The identity of the creator is imprinted on creation. It is an identity that expresses relationship. Some important aspects of God's act of creation help us understand the nature of God's relationship to the world.

1 God, creation and the other

First, God's act of creation is primarily an attitude of openness to the other. It is God's affirmation of the other. It makes possible the other in relation to God's Self. Perhaps it was not necessary at all for God to have created an other. God would still be God and could well exist without a creation. Yet, as we see in Genesis 1, the presence of the other evokes joy. God repeatedly finds creation good.

Creation is not an act on its own. It needs the Creator and an object to be created. 'Saying' (or speaking) and 'seeing' are two actions we find again and again in God's act of creation. Both are actions of relationship from one to an other. Saying presupposes that there is already a receiver. Of course, the text does not reveal the manner of God's speaking. One may say that God was speaking only to Godself. However, in that speaking a relationship is formed, not primarily with the Self, but with a wholly other. Here the other receives God's words and responds to them accordingly, and thus a mutual relationship is formed. Similarly, seeing is a matter of relating with the other, of relating with an object. God sees everything that God has created and sees it as good, and a healthy relationship is affirmed.

2 Creation, difference and diversity

Another important aspect of God's act is that it is an affirmation of difference and diversity in God's creation. We know that acknowledging our differences and celebrating diversity are foundational to relationships. Here God is creating – and clearly appreciates – difference and diversity. In this regard, let us consider some of the other actions of God in the process of creation.

First, separation: in Genesis 1, we see acts of separation again and again. God separates the light from the darkness (verses 4, 18). God makes a dome to separate the waters from the waters (verses 6, 7). God separates the day from the night (verse 14). Here God's act of separation is not to put the one in opposition to the other, but to keep one *different* from the other. God is not dividing something and throwing away one part while keeping the other. Both water and land are to exist. Both physical darkness and light are necessary; their recurrence contributes to the existence of the world, keeping it moving. The act of separation marks the importance of difference and the necessity of diversity. Indeed it is an affirmation of both.

Second, naming and calling: naming distinct things is an important process in creation, and God enters into it passionately and with great enjoyment! There is an attachment between the one who names and the one who is named. When we go to Genesis 2, God takes a special interest in seeing how Adam will name the creatures in the world. Verse 19 says:

> So out of the ground the LORD God formed every animal of the field and every bird of the air, and brought them to the man to see what he would call them; and whatever the man called every living creature, that was its name.

We do not know how Adam named the creatures, though it is interesting to see that the next verse (20) underlines the connection between naming and relationships:

> The man gave names to all cattle, and to the birds of the air, and to every animal of the field; *but* for the man there was not found a helper as his partner.

'But' is an interesting word here. The man gives names to every other creature and relates to them, but he does not have a partner with whom he can form an intimate bond (we shall return to this shortly). Naming is closely connected with relationships, although when it is done from a dominant position towards the other – as often happens in our world today – it has the power to exclude and discriminate against those whom we don't see as 'insiders'. Nonetheless, in God's act of creation, naming establishes the importance of difference and thus affirms the significance of diversity.

3 Creation and the interdependence of creatures

God's creation is not simply about adding more and more elements, but about relating these one with another – sometimes by making one element produce another, sometimes through separating them in such a way that they both work in relation to the other.

In Genesis 1.11 we see that the land puts forth vegetation. The earth relates to vegetation by producing it and vegetation in turn relates to and depends upon the earth. Similarly, the waters bring forth swarms of living creatures (verse 20) and the earth brings forth living creatures (verse 24). God blesses the creatures, saying 'be fruitful and multiply' (verse 22), which is basically a command to enter into relationship and interdependence. In chapter 2.18, God recognizes the need for human dependence on another human being: 'it is not good that the man should be alone.' Thus, God makes sure that the relationships initiated with the creation continue though interdependence among the creation.

God's act of creation says everything about forming, making, building and maintaining relationships. God is pleased about the existence of the other in relation to God's self. God blesses difference and diversity in creation, then makes the elements of creation relate with, and be mutually dependent upon, one another. It is apparent that conciliation and reconciliation are part of God's plan in creation itself, although they are manifested in particular concrete forms later in specific events, like those recorded in Genesis 3.

When we think about God's involvement in the world, we do consider creation, but we rush to talk about the fall. Thus, we neglect to notice the effort God voluntarily takes through the act of creation to nurture relationships and hence reconciliation. The point is that you don't need to wait until the fall to think about why God reconciles the world: God's openness to relationship and God's *proactive* creation of relationship is the beginning of reconciliation.

How does this fit with the work of Jesus Christ? That is what we shall consider next.

Questions for reflection

1 How does pondering the interdependence of things – human beings on God, human beings on one another and human beings on creation and vice versa – help us understand the importance of reconciliation?
2 Creation is God's simple affirmation of diversity. Reflect on this.
3 What lessons can we learn from God's open and positive attitude towards the other?

3 Jesus Christ: reconciling us with God and with one another

Key themes:
- The Word becoming flesh
- Emmanuel
- God becoming slave
- Jesus the mediator

The ultimate purpose of the incarnation of Christ, as we know, is to reconcile us with God (2 Corinthians 5.17–20; Colossians 1.19–22), and to reconcile us with one another (Ephesians 2.14–16). Yet the process of reconciling us with God was not a simple one, even for Christ. It was a painful process. It was a journey that involved rejection, contempt and lack of acceptance among his own people, suffering, and ultimately the cross. Though nothing would deter Jesus from bringing the joy of reconciliation to us.

Jesus' ministry of reconciliation might be described as both vertical and horizontal. Through his incarnation he broke the boundaries between God and the world that human sin had constructed. In his life and ministry, he crossed many of the borders that existed in his society. Radical openness toward the other defined his life and work. Leaving his position of being equal to God, he became vulnerable and identified with the vulnerable in order to save them. He continues his ministry of reconciliation by standing in between God and us and mediating for us to God.

1 Breaking boundaries: the Word becoming flesh

Jesus' ministry of breaking boundaries begins with his very coming into the world. We read in John 1.14 that the incarnation of Christ was 'the Word becoming flesh.' The Word and the flesh belong to different realms. One is eternal and the other temporal. One is Spirit and the other is matter. Breaking the boundaries between them is possible only for Christ.

As in his incarnation, Jesus breaks boundaries throughout his life and ministry. He breaks the boundaries between God and human beings. He breaks the boundaries among human beings and communities. His challenging of physical, social, cultural and religious norms was unthinkable and quite unacceptable at such a time. He often goes to 'enemy' territories (for instance, Mark 7). He moves freely among sinners. He heals lepers, the lame and the blind. No boundary ever mattered for Christ. It took time for his disciples to catch on, but Jesus often invited or challenged them to do as he was doing. Breaking boundaries and crossing borders to reconcile alienated human beings with God, and hostile communities with one another, is an essential part of following Christ.

Jesus' way of disciple-making was not simply asking people to follow him. He called his disciples from different backgrounds and cultures, and their attitudes to one another could be unfriendly. Quite often the disciples find it difficult to accept and reconcile with one another. Jesus makes this a challenge for them, and the disciples slowly learn to love and live together.

As in his birth, his life and his ministry, Jesus breaks boundaries through his death: the thick curtain of the temple is torn in two (Matthew 27.51), which means we can now relate directly to God. And in his resurrection, Jesus breaks the boundaries between death and life, and assures us, his followers, of new life.

2 Embracing differences: Emmanuel, God with us

Another image of Christ that is closely associated with his function as a reconciler between God and the world is Emmanuel – God with us (Matthew 1.23). God's relationship with the world, which began in creation, continues through the coming of Emmanuel. From God creating the other, celebrating its existence and initiating a relationship with it, we move to Christ embracing and identifying with the difference between the Creator and God's creation, and coming to live permanently with human beings as Emmanuel.

Jesus Christ has brought God, who was once considered far off, down to us and close to us, and now God wants to dwell in us permanently. Jesus' coming expresses God's will to be eternally related to us. Jesus embodies the embracing of difference, which is foundational to building relationships. He has demonstrated to us the importance of openness to the other, and how to work at this difficult task.

3 Reconciliation through cross, not power: God becoming slave

Another feature of Jesus Christ the reconciler is expressed though God becoming a slave in order to identify with the vulnerable (Philippians

2.6–8). Leaving power and privilege, he shows the means by which he will undertake his ministry of reconciliation: not by might but through the cross. The way to reconciliation involves servanthood and suffering, rather than power.

4 Jesus the mediator

During his ministry, Jesus prayed for his disciples, for unity between them (John 17), and for the church to come. He continues his work of reconciliation by identifying with the vulnerable and mediating to God for us (Hebrews 8.6, 9.15, 12.24; I Timothy 2.5).

Through his incarnation, life, ministry and by being eternally with human beings:

Jesus has reconciled God and sinners;

Jesus has reconciled the Jews and the Gentiles;

Jesus has reconciled hostile communities;

Jesus has reconciled the marginalized and powerful, through the latter doing justice to the former;

Jesus continues to reconcile us with God through mediating for us.

Questions for reflection

1 It is an essential part of the nature of God to break boundaries. Why is this?

2 Jesus is Emmanuel, 'God with us', but we often behave as if God is far away rather than close to us. How can we overcome this tendency? How might it be affecting our reconciliation ministry?

3 To reconcile through the cross is not an easy thing. What are the challenges you face when you work for reconciliation this way?

4 Holy Spirit, the reconciler

Key themes:
- The Holy Spirit reconciling us with God
- The Holy Spirit helping to cross boundaries in mission
- The Holy Spirit as unity and bond of the Christian community

When Jesus ascended to heaven, his disciples were not left alone. Jesus promised the Holy Spirit, and during the last 20 centuries, the Holy Spirit has been leading the Church, continuing the reconciliation ministry of Jesus Christ throughout the world. Some of the roles of the Holy Spirit, as explained by the earliest church in the New Testament, are reconciling us with God; enabling Christians to cross boundaries and bring together divided communities; and strengthening relationships and bonds in the Christian community.

1 The Holy Spirit reconciles us with God

The Holy Spirit continues the work of Jesus Christ by proving 'the world wrong about sin and righteousness and judgment' (John 16.8). This function of the Holy Spirit is crucial in the work of reconciliation. As counsellor, the Holy Spirit helps us mend and deepen our relationship with God amidst the stresses and strains of everyday Christian living. In the Bible, the Holy Spirit is often associated with oneness and the work of uniting believers.

The Holy Spirit also continues the function of Emmanuel – God with us. Paul, in his many epistles, talks about the in-dwelling nature of the Spirit (1 Corinthians 3.16, 6.19; 2 Timothy 1.14; Romans 8.9,11; Galatians 4.6). Jesus promised his disciples that the Holy Spirit would abide with the followers of Christ for ever (John 14.16). By in-dwelling us, the Holy Spirit continues and sustains the relationship between God and the world.

Further, as Jesus did, the Holy Spirit mediates between us and God. We read in Romans 8.26–27 that the Holy Spirit prays and intercedes for us. Intercession and mediation are crucial in reconciling sinners with God and believers in the community with one another, and the Holy Spirit's involvement encourages vibrancy and growth.

2 The Holy Spirit reconciles hostile communities

The Holy Spirit makes reconciliation possible, not only between God and human beings, but also among hostile communities. There are a number of such instances in the Bible. In the Book of Acts, the Holy Spirit is first spoken of in the context of the mission of the disciples of Christ to *connect* the people on the earth by being witnesses to Christ.

Acts 1.6–8, one of the foundational texts on mission and the last words of Jesus Christ to his disciples before he ascends into heaven, is also about reconciliation. Jesus talks about what kind of mission would take place when the Holy Spirit comes upon the disciples. It will be a mission not simply of propagation, but also of reconciliation.

In this text, the disciples ask Jesus questions about the time when Christ will restore the kingdom to Israel. Jesus, after a rebuke that this is not for them to know, says:

> But you will receive power when the Holy Spirit has come upon you; and you will be my witnesses in Jerusalem, in all Judea and Samaria, and to the ends of the earth. (Acts 1.6–8)

The disciples want the power that isolates, but Jesus contrasts this with the power of the Holy Spirit that will help reconcile. When the Holy Spirit empowers them, the disciples will no longer be concerned primarily with the kingdom of Israel; rather, they will be galvanized to witness to people all over the world. They will do this not only by travelling from Jerusalem, but by *being witnesses* in Jerusalem, in Judea and Samaria, and to the ends of the earth. This text does not simply command mission (in the sense of going out). Mission is not only proclamation in the sense of telling those who do not know Jesus about him. Wherever we participate in the mission of God, we are involved in building relationships with the peoples and the cultures of that place. This is an important part of mission. Witnessing in regions that are in conflict involves boundary-crossing and reconciliation.

When the Holy Spirit empowers them, the disciples will be witnesses in Judea and Samaria. It is not accidental that these two regions are mentioned together. Jesus struggles hard for reconciliation between Judea and Samaria during his ministry, and now the Holy Spirit is entering into this work through the witnessing of the disciples. When the Holy Spirit comes, it will be possible to bring together Judea and Samaria, to build relationships between hostile people and communities.

In our Christian life, we are often aware that the Holy Spirit is not bound by time, space and human boundaries, and the New

Testament church experienced this too. We see the Holy Spirit as reconciler between the Jews and the Gentiles in the Peter-Cornelius story in Acts 10. Peter is preaching to the Gentiles gathered at the house of Cornelius when the Holy Spirit falls on them. Peter may not have expected this, in spite of going to Cornelius and acknowledging that God is not partial (verse 34). Those who accompanied Peter definitely did not expect this! We read that:

> While Peter was still speaking, the Holy Spirit fell upon all who heard the word. The circumcised believers who had come with Peter were astounded that the gift of the Holy Spirit had been poured out even on the Gentiles. (Acts 10.44–45)

'Even on the Gentiles' clearly indicates that the disciples still had some boundaries in place, but the Holy Spirit is not bound by these. Reconciliation between the Jews and the Gentiles is a recurring theme in Paul's epistles too, and when writing to the Ephesians, he says that both Jews and Gentiles have access in one Spirit to the Father (2.18).

3 The Holy Spirit strengthens the bonds in the Christian community

To make our Christian life a life in community, the Holy Spirit's ministry of reconciliation strengthens relationships between the followers of Christ. Paul repeatedly speaks of the in-dwelling nature of the Holy Spirit as defining what Christian community is (Romans 8.23; Ephesians 4.3–4; Philippians 2.1). For him, the Spirit is unity (Ephesians 4.3–4) and we are to live in oneness of Spirit:

> But you are not in the flesh; you are in the Spirit, since the Spirit of God dwells in you. Anyone who does not have the Spirit of Christ does not belong to him. (Romans 8.9)

Paul also talks about the fruit of the Spirit in his epistle to Galatians. He says:

> The fruit of the Spirit is love, joy, peace, patience, kindness, generosity, faithfulness, gentleness, and self-control. There is no law against such things. And those who belong to Christ Jesus have crucified the flesh with its passions and desires. If we live by the Spirit, let us also be guided by the Spirit. Let us not become conceited, competing against one another, envying one another. (Galatians 5.22–26)

The values which are mentioned here are all essential for building and maintaining relationships with God and with our fellow human beings. Love, joy, peace, patience, kindness, generosity, faithfulness, gentleness and self-control are closely connected to reconciliation and relationships in a community and are essential for mending relationships when they break down.

We can rejoice that the Holy Spirit allows diversity in a community, yet unifies it, because it is the same Spirit (1 Corinthians 12.4). The Holy Spirit is the giver of spiritual gifts – different gifts to different people, but the Spirit is one. Difference and diversity in exercising the gifts of the Spirit need not lead to conflict, but can be the basis for building bridges.

Thus, as Christians participating in the ministry of reconciliation, we have the Holy Spirit, the reconciler, with us. The Holy Spirit continues the task of Jesus in reconciling us with God. The Holy Spirit removes the boundaries between communities and helps us to move beyond enmity and reconcile with one another. The Spirit ensures diversity yet unity in the Christian community.

Questions for reflection

1 Recollect moments in your life when the Holy Spirit has enabled you to reconcile with God and with one another.
2 How does the Holy Spirit, as the one who moves 'in between', help us in our mission activities?
3 The Spirit-filled life is essential for the ministry of reconciliation. Reflect on this.

5 The Church: reconciliation within and reconciliation in the world

Key themes:

- The Church is fellowship
- The Church is an inclusive community
- The Church needs to be self-critical
- The Church's ministry of reconciliation

My conversion to Christianity was primarily based on experiencing a church community that modelled living for Christ. When I was seven, some of my church-going friends invited me to their church. It was relaxing going with them and I started to enjoy it. One fine Sunday after the worship service, I was at Sunday school when the pastor asked me if I was interested in going to church regularly. If I wished, he would put my name in the Sunday school register. Four decades ago in my culture, an adult rarely asked a person so young if he 'wished' to do anything. I didn't have my parents to consult and really wasn't sure what to say, but I thought: every Sunday after the service, people gather casually in front of the church, smile and converse with one another and with me too. This may seem a normal thing, but I find it pleasant and welcoming. It shows me what the Church of Christ is, and I feel part of a fellowship and community. So I said to the pastor, yes, I want to continue to come. I have always regarded this as the moment I committed my life to Christ.

In other words, my conversion was based on what happened at church, where people witnessed to Christ and were kind and caring towards others in the fellowship, rather than on Christian doctrine or Bible verses about ultimate truth. I have continued to reflect on the attractiveness of an attitude of welcome and fellowship in a church, arising from the love of God shown to humanity through Christ. Indeed, St Augustine, one of the greatest theologians of the Church, tells of how on his journey the warm welcome he received from St Ambrose, Bishop of Milan, drew him to Christ. This eventually led him to conversion and baptism by Ambrose:

> So I came to Milan to Bishop Ambrose, who was known throughout the world as one of the best of men. He was a devout worshipper of you, Lord, and at that time, his energetic preaching provided your people with choicest wheat and the joy of oil and the sober

intoxication of wine . . . This man of God welcomed me with fairly kindness and showed the charitable concern for my pilgrimage that befitted a bishop. *I began to feel affection for him, not first as a teacher of truth . . . but simply as a man who was kind to me.*

(St. Augustine, *Confessions,* 5.13, 23, emphasis added)

Today, decline in the Church is something we hear about quite often, particularly among Christians in the West. It is a contested topic, as some say churches in the majority world are actually growing. Some challenge the very definition of decline – whether it should be assessed qualitatively or quantitatively. While this is too complex an issue to have a single answer, we Christians often cite secularism or secularization as the enemy. This baffles me! Many of us have what we call secular values, as do our churches and traditions. The values that we despise as secular actually do not exist outside us, though we do not have the courage to admit this. Also, whether a religious-secular distinction, as used in our contemporary context, is tenable is a topic discussed a lot in contemporary research in religious studies. I do not propose to go into it here, but I do feel we can blame the secular and fail to see where the Church itself has gone wrong in not being welcoming enough towards others.

The Church is a gift of God: through Christ we are in fellowship with God and with one another (Ephesians 2.19–22; Colossians 3.14). We are to show commitment and responsibility towards one another (Galatians 6.10; Romans 12.5; 1 Corinthians 12.27; Ephesians 4.16). If we remove the fellowship and community aspect of the Church, it ceases to exist. It is a reconciled community – reconciled by Jesus Christ with God – that is charged to reconcile others with God and with one another, and to invite others to be part of it. For being a church means being there for others (Philippians 2.1–4). It means being open to others. It means being responsible for others.

Although the Church is a gift of God and God wants it to be a body that unifies believers in fellowship, it has experienced conflicts and divisions within from the very beginning. Some of the New Testament epistles urge reconciliation in churches where there is conflict: letters to the Corinthians, Galatians, Ephesians and Philippines mostly discuss this concern, and many of the other epistles also talk about conflicting situations in Christian communities and how to address and resolve them. The Church has never been perfect, but by continuously seeking reconciliation with God and with one another, its members grow as a community. The ministry of reconciliation has been entrusted to them.

What are the most important aspects of the Christian ministry of reconciliation? Today Christian reconciliation involves the following:

1 Christians reconciling with one another in their local churches or congregations, including their immediate communities and starting with their families.
2 Christians seeking reconciliation between denominations within the Church.
3 Christians seeking reconciliation with people of other religions and traditions.
4 Christians seeking to reconcile with society, addressing the traditional religion versus society clash.
5 Christians seeking to reconcile those who are in conflict with one another – and repenting of supporting conflicts in society itself.

We often find ourselves in need of the ministry of reconciliation for and among ourselves. It is important, first, to maintain and strengthen the relationships within our local churches – among the members, between clergy and laity, and between those who administer and the rest. Given the importance to society of the witness of the local church, proper relationships within these churches are essential. We cannot always blame secularization, atheism and related ideologies if we seem to be lacking in relevance.

Second, the centuries-old divisions between various churches and denominations need to be addressed. Fortunately, we have become increasingly aware of the need for proper relationship and cooperation. Ecumenical relationships may require much effort and sacrifice on the part of the participants, but they help us keep looking outward rather than becoming rigid and self-absorbed. They are highly important for the existence of the Church and its witness today, though we have a long way to go.

Third, we find ourselves living in close proximity to people from other religions, traditions and ideologies. 'Christian relations with non-Christian religions' has been a dominant theme in our missionary endeavours for more than a century now. However, we still have a lot of work to do in creating and maintaining open attitudes towards our neighbours from other religions and ideologies. It is impossible to talk about Christian witness and relevance nowadays without addressing this particular issue.

Fourth, reconciliation is significant in the context of the Church's relations with society. I don't subscribe to the view that there is a thick wall dividing these – we Christians live in society and 'social' cannot be explained away from us. Nevertheless, there are Christians who consider society as something from which the religious and spiritual should be segregated. The relationship between church and society is one of the most significant topics in Christian thinking, and in the context of the Christian ministry of reconciliation, working for better relationships between them is important and urgent.

Finally, Christians are entrusted with the task of resolving conflicts between different groups and communities and building relationships between them. Taking this proactive step follows the example set by our Lord; it is part of our responsibility to protect God's creation and to build God's kingdom. The significance of Christian reconciliation lies in the fact that we can effectively build bridges, create friendships and exercise hospitality in a world which is tormented by conflicts, but which needs reconciliation and proper relationships for its existence.

Questions for reflection

1 Why do we need to consider our own behaviour more than the impact of outside forces in understanding the decline of the Church today? In what ways can we encourage healthy self-examination?

2 Is there really a church-society divide? How might we address pertinent issues while avoiding (unhelpful) binary thinking?

3 What is the purpose of being a church in a community?

3

Impediments to reconciliation

Reconciliation is a very soothing and pleasing word, but the process of building and re-building relationships is challenging. There are many impediments to reconciliation in our personal, spiritual and community life and these are often not easy to overcome.

Obviously we need to have an awareness of any existing hindrances if we are to participate in reconciliation ministry effectively. We should constantly be asking questions such as: why do I have difficulty relating to this other person? What stops us reconciling?

In this chapter we reflect on impediments to reconciliation such as passing on the blame to others, prejudice and stereotyping, wealth and greed, using silence to stop the betterment of others, rushing to judge others, false reconciliation, and dragging on a conflict in spite of someone apologizing for their mistakes.

6 Passing on the blame to others: different from the 'original' sin?

Key text: Genesis 3
The first sin!

If the conversation between God, Adam and Eve in the Garden of Eden had been different, would that have changed humanity's journey through this world? Would it have changed God's relationships with human beings? Yes? No? We simply can't tell.

Adam and Eve disobey God's commandment and sin against God. The omniscient and omnipresent God obviously knows what has happened; he knows that Adam and Eve are hiding. Yet God 'searches' for them and visits them to have a conversation. God didn't need to act in this way to punish them, but perhaps hoped Adam and Eve would take responsibility for what they had done, instead of passing the blame on to others. I often think this might have been the case.

The narrative may appear to suggest that, in eating the fruit, Adam and Eve committed the original sin, but it becomes clear during the course of conversation with God that this act is indicative of a deeper malaise. In fact, what happens in Eden is that there is a breakdown for the first time in the God–human relationship because of something that human beings have done. Connected to this is the first ever breakdown in the relationship between two individuals. The latter is not simply the consequence of the former, they are wholly interconnected.

In the responses of Adam and Eve to God, we see each attempting to protect the self against the other in ways that are clearly detrimental to the couple's relationship. Verses 10 to 13 reveal their attitudes to each other and we can identify at least three problems here.

Exclusion

First, in Adam's reply to God there is a clear attitude of exclusion. 'We' language is completely missing. Look at the number of times the word 'I' is used. We find it four times, and along with the use of 'myself' Adam's response is fully in the first person singular. 'I' is at the centre, but this does not reflect reality. Verse 8 clearly says 'they' hear the sound of the Lord God walking in the garden and 'they' hide themselves. Adam has forgotten he is part of a 'we'. He is concerned only with himself. He talks only about *his* hearing the sound of God, *his* fear, *his* nakedness and *his* hiding, although Adam and Eve experienced all these things jointly. This attitude of exclusion is no less sinful than eating the fruit.

Othering

Second, Adam's response reveals an attitude of 'othering' someone with whom he is fully connected. Speaking to God in verse 12, he refers to his wife Eve as 'the woman you gave me.' What a sad sense of disowning! In only the previous chapter we read his ecstatic, 'This at last is bone of my bones and flesh of my flesh; this one shall be called Woman, for out of Man this one was taken' (2.23). Yet here Adam fails to acknowledge Eve as his own and, in the process, indirectly blames God for what has gone wrong.

Perhaps if we were to compare religions (although there may be a risk of generalization here), we would conclude that Christianity, being rooted in both the Old and the New Testaments, promotes one of the most important concepts of all: that human beings are created in the image of God. This world view is fundamentally opposed to taking even a small step to disown our fellow human beings. Nevertheless, a negative attitude of othering is evident very early on; it is quickly adopted by the very first human beings.

Passing on the blame

Third, in the responses of both Adam and Eve to God, we come across an attitude of accusing the other, rather than realizing, admitting to and confessing a fault. Adam avoids a direct answer to God's question, 'Have you eaten from the tree of which I commanded you not to eat?' The answer should simply be 'yes', but Adam brings Eve into the equation rather than take responsibility for his own mistake. After all, any error on his part was only the result of what she did. An understanding of how Adam actively participated in the mistake is missing.

The most serious problem with accusing others when we make mistakes is that we lose sight of the need for self-interrogation or self-criticism. We rush to protect our own self. Avoiding the role of 'I' is the first step in putting the blame on the other. As a result of doing this, Adam blames Eve, and Eve blames the serpent. The story perfectly depicts the way in which human beings react to threats. This kind of attitude may be seen today as a driving force in almost all conflicts, wars and genocides among communities, ethnic groups and nations.

When expressing his fears (verse 10) and projecting himself as a victim (verse 12), Adam excludes his wife. When he finally refers to her, he disconnects from her. When he has to talk about his mistake, Adam presents Eve as its cause, suggesting his action is only the result of what she has done. He tries to distance himself from the seriousness of his sin. Eve does the same with the serpent. In fact, Adam should talk about Eve's fears and experiences rather than only his own, and both should confess their own faults, rather than talking about the faults of the other.

Our human tendency is to believe that if something good happens, it is always because of us, and if something bad happens, it is always because of others. This is very detrimental to community life and the building of relationships. Words like 'I have made a mistake' and 'I have made a mistake too' go a long way to ease the process of reconciliation.

The narration of the first sin in Genesis 3 tells us not only that disobedience and lack of trust in God adversely affect our relationship with God, but also that sin should be understood against the background of spoiled human relations – and that spoiled human relations can affect reconciliation. In our troubled world, questions such as 'why does violence happens?', 'why do people kill one another?' and 'why is there so much hate?' often prompt us to consider the roots of these evils in human sin. In such a context, the conversation between God, Adam and Eve – where we see the attitudes of exclusion, othering and passing on the blame in order to protect one's self – can help us to identify and reflect on the roots of the problems and conflicts in human relations, which cannot be separated from the first sin in the Garden of Eden.

Questions for reflection

1　Why is blaming others and not being self-critical unhelpful in reconciliation?
2　Reflect on some of the ways in which we practise excluding others, othering those we are close to, and passing on blame to others.
3　Do you think if Adam and Eve had admitted their sin instead of accusing the other, God's relationship with humanity would have been different?

7 Prejudice and stereotyping

Key text: John 1.45-51
Can anything good come good out of Nazareth?

Two of the major stumbling blocks to building and maintaining relationships with others are prejudice and stereotyping. In this study we look at how these are impeding progress in reconciliation work in our world today.

Prejudice is holding a preconceived opinion about something without actually knowing or experiencing or being part of it. It usually relates to a group of people, whether a nation, an ethnic community or a particular religion. We tend to assume that something is bad (although prejudice may also lead us to assume it is good). Generally, we have a prejudice *against* something that we consider inferior to what we are, or what we have, or what we like. Even for people committed to equality and justice, prejudice and stereotyping are not easy to overcome.

Basic to prejudice and stereotyping is naming. Naming is not innocent: it defines the relationship between the one who names and the one who is named. If one names an other from a dominant position, it will affect the relationship between them. There will be a sense of inclusion and exclusion.

Prejudice and stereotyping involve generalization. For instance, based on one (or a few) encounter(s), we tend to form an opinion of people and where they come from. If we have been cheated in a particular shop or hotel in a city, it's quite easy to think badly about the entire place. You may hear people say things like, 'I was ridiculously overcharged by the taxi driver taking me from the airport to my hotel – I'll never go there again!' It's undeniable that we have many preconceived and generalized opinions about people who are different from us. In a world context, linking Islam blindly with terrorism – as if the whole of Islam is encouraging violence or as if all Muslims are terrorists – is one of the best examples of how prejudice and stereotyping operate in our lives.

Although these negative tendencies may be part of our everyday experience, we must not underrate how dangerous and detrimental they are. It can take a long time to heal broken relationships between people and between communities because we struggle so much to overcome negative ways of thinking about one another.

Prejudice is also often associated with how we cope with difference between us and an other. This is a self and other relational issue, and the problem comes when we ascribe a value to the difference. Seeing something and saying it is different is not prejudice, whereas seeing something and saying it is bad may well be.

Many people could not reconcile with Jesus, his followers and his message because they were prejudiced in some way. The Jewish leaders of his day had problems with where Jesus came from and simply couldn't overcome this bias.

In John 1.45–46 we see an interesting conversation between Philip, who has just joined Jesus' disciples, and Nathaniel. Philip says, 'We have found him about whom Moses in the law and also the prophets wrote, Jesus son of Joseph from Nazareth.' Nathaniel's immediate reaction is 'can anything good come out of Nazareth?'

We know little about Nazareth before the time of Jesus as it is not mentioned in the Hebrew Scriptures. As a result, some think Nazareth was a very insignificant village, and to hear it being undermined by Jewish leaders would hardly be surprising. It may have been on a Roman trade route and associated with immorality, so despised for that.

Either way, it is apparent that Nathaniel is prejudiced against Nazareth and, thus, Jesus because he comes from Nazareth. His comment may have arisen because of the prevalent belief in Judea, based on the prophecy of Micah, that the Messiah will come from Bethlehem (Micah 5.2). It may be understandable that he is puzzled about how the Messiah could be from Nazareth, given what the prophets have said, but Nathaniel's question is not 'Can the Messiah come from Nazareth?', but 'can *anything* good come out of Nazareth?' The implied answer is obviously no – nothing good can come from Nazareth; the whole town should be written off. When we compare this incident with that in John 7, where the Jewish leaders reply to Nicodemus (who says they should first listen to Jesus before charging him), 'Surely you are not also from Galilee, are you? Search and you will see that no prophet is to arise from Galilee', we can clearly see the prejudice against and stereotyping of Nazareth and Galilee. These negative attitudes stood in the way of many people around Jesus accepting him and what he was doing.

Note that Philip does not argue with or chastise Nathaniel. He simply asks him to 'Come and see'. These are very powerful words.

Prejudice can be overcome when you 'come and see' rather than stay away. Nathaniel's prejudice soon dissipates (verse 47).

As Jesus already knows Nathaniel, he is aware of his world view, so his attitude when he meets the new disciple is one of understanding. He doesn't accuse him of prejudice or stereotyping, but calls him innocent. Being categorized is hurtful, but Jesus shows that it is important to try to understand those who make generalized judgements. He reminds us here that if we try to understand the one who is prejudiced against us, we shall be better able to relate with them.

Of course, not all conversations and disputes based on prejudice have as happy an ending as that between Nathaniel and Jesus. In our time, we most often see them leading to further conflict.

What we learn from this text is that prejudice against others and stereotyping them is wrong and dangerous. Perhaps second only to the desire for power and wealth in effect, prejudice and stereotyping cause many conflicts, particularly between communities, nations and cultures. They often stand in the way of efforts towards reconciliation, but if new relationships are to be formed and old ones renewed and strengthened, they must be overcome.

We need to learn not to react badly towards difference. Acknowledging difference (which is highly important for human diversity) is distinct from discriminating against it, based on language, region, religion or ethnicity.

Like Nathaniel, are we ready to go and see? Are we ready to experience the other? Are we ready to overcome our prejudice and stereotyping in order to make reconciliation work?

Questions for reflection

1 What are some of the ways in which the Bible teaches us to overcome prejudice against the other and to avoid stereotyping based on our personal bias?
2 Have you ever identified the prejudices you have uncritically accepted against other individuals and communities? What steps have you taken to overcome them?
3 How might we experience the other?

8 Wealth, greed and conflict

Key texts: Genesis 13
Wealth separating Abram and Lot

If we were to identify some of the main reasons for clashes between individuals, communities and nations generally, ego, power and wealth might come top of the list (although we are more likely to use terms such as religious, ethnic or national conflict). In this study, we look at a story in the Bible in which wealth was a reason for conflict – and did not, in any way, help in the process of reconciliation.

One of the driving forces behind the urge for economic growth is the notion that increased well-being can improve relationships and make the world a better place. Wealth creation may present the opportunity to eradicate poverty among the poor and bring about greater equality. These ideas probably do make some people's lives richer and more sophisticated, but do they solve inequality and dissolve conflict among people and groups? The answer is before our eyes. It appears very much as if economic development leads to greater inequality and more conflict. If the ego is largely responsible for the breakdown of personal relationships, and the struggle for power causes damage in the social and political arena, it is wealth and greed that are behind many of the conflicts in the world today. Of course, wealth and power often go together, as Paul says so succinctly: 'the love of money is a root of all kinds of evil' (1 Timothy 6.10).

In Genesis 13, wealth comes between two men related by blood, Abram and his brother's son, Lot. The struggle between Esau and Jacob (which we will study later) is another story of wealth and greed causing ructions in a brotherly relationship. While there is some sort of reconciliation between Esau and Jacob, we don't see this happen here. In fact, it is the availability of wealth and the desire for more that prevents any reconciliation between Abram and Lot. The Psalmist says, 'How very good and pleasant it is when kindred live together in unity!' (Psalm 133.1), but here the men prefer to separate in order to grow even richer.

Verse 6 says that 'the land could not support both of them living together; for their possessions were so great that they could not live together.' The land could not support them? Or their wealth could not? One might say separation is necessary in order to fulfil the promise of God's blessing to Abram and his descendants. Yet the conflict and separation lead to more problems for Lot and his family. Sometimes there seems to be a tendency to say this is his own fault, but it is Abram who bears more responsibility. He offers the solution of separation because this will make more wealth available.

1 Where is God?

Wealth affects Abram and Lot in such a way that God's help is not sought by either of them in their conflict. God just disappears from the story. God, who has promised and actually given all these blessings, is nowhere to be seen. A short time ago, Abram needed God in his difficulty with Pharaoh, and we read of several others times when, for various reasons, Abram goes to God, interacts with God and seeks God's guidance. Yet in his strife over wealth with his own nephew, he fails to turn to God. Nor does Lot seek God's help.

The availability of wealth is referred to again and again in the conversation between Abram and Lot. However, they do not acknowledge that this is God's blessing; both prefer to treat what is available as their own, rather than graciously given by God. In his book *Dethroning Mammon: Making Money Serve Grace*, Archbishop Justin Welby reflects that one of the problems of wealth in our life is that 'what we receive we treat as ours'. Both Abram and Lot fall into the trap. This is a fundamental problem.

In conflicts that benefit us, we don't need God. In conflicts that secure us wealth, we don't need God. In the history of Christianity in the West, when many Bible-practising Christians were trading slaves and owning them as property, they didn't need God. When wars benefit our economy and the sale of arms benefits our nation, we don't need God. What we do want is a God who will not mind how we accumulate and preserve our wealth, even if it is at the cost of tension and relational breakdown in society.

2 Our servants' problem is our problem?

We see that the problems Abram and Lot experience originate from fighting between their servants. They could have decided that this dispute would not come between them; that they were relatives who could work together to sort things out. Yet due to wealth, the conflicts between the servants become their conflicts.

3 Separation as a solution!

Abram and Lot do actually come together to speak about the problem. They want to solve it, but how? Abram seems to present a positive face and offer a suggestion to end the trouble, but he doesn't actually work for reconciliation. Rather, he proposes to Lot that separation should be an option. Abram wants good to happen, but he is not willing to solve the problem that is making it difficult for them to stay together. The understanding is that if they separate, the conflict will disappear. Abram allows the wealth in view to make the divide even deeper. He says to Lot,

> Is not the whole land before you? Separate yourself from me. If you take the left hand, then I will go to the right; or if you take the right hand, then I will go to the left. (verse 9)

Living together becomes a problem for the relatives. We often experience proximity as a factor in conflicts. The next door neighbour, the family across the road, the village close to ours, the nations whose borders we share, can be a real problem; and jealousy and hatred may arise particularly when somebody close to us has great riches. Embarrassingly, it is very easy to talk graciously to – and feel warmth towards – a friend who is far away; less easy with our immediate neighbours! Both Abram and Lot should have seen proximity as a blessing, but Abram suggests separation as a solution and Lot accepts this. He does not say, why don't we solve the conflict and stay together?

4 Wealth not only creates conflicts, it blocks any attempt at reconciliation

The availability of great wealth means that the relatives feel less pressure to solve their problems. When they come together in conversation, it seems a reconciliation is possible between them, but the richness of the resources around them mean they can separate. Wealth in this instance simply effects greater division. Verse 10 says that 'Lot looked about him, and saw that the plain of the Jordan was well watered everywhere like the garden of the LORD, like the land of Egypt, in the direction of Zoar.' The strife seems to have dissipated, but in fact, Abram and Lot have failed to solve anything.

Jesus often spoke about how wealth gets in the way in relationships, whether between us and God or in the relationships we have with one another. In Matthew 19.21–22, the rich man goes away sad because he has many possessions. It seems that great wealth never helps to make relationships better.

A desire for economic superiority, or having a vested interest in power, can lead to conflict. Acts 19 tells of how, fearing economic loss, a silversmith in Ephesus named Demetrius leads the people around him to riot against Paul and his associates. Perhaps this is a classic example of how conflict – whether religious, national or racial – is primarily concerned with protecting and attaining economic resources.

Human beings want to become rich and richer, but usually, as one becomes richer, one is unable to work with and relate well to others. Neo-capitalism claims that it can solve economic inequality by creating more wealth in order to help the poor, but creating wealth has led to great environmental destruction and has caused millions of poor people to become displaced. Equality has never come. Only conflict and broken relationships seem to have been the result.

Questions for reflection

1 Do you think your riches have affected your relationships with others?
2 Have you made a small conflict between you and someone, which could have been solved easily, into a more serious one?
3 In what ways might our wealth be utilized for reconciliation and building relationships in society rather being a stumbling block?

9 Being silent when we have to speak and act

Key text: Luke 14.1–6
When our silence is against Jesus Christ's ministry of
reconciliation

Imagine you are in a church and the sermon is just about to begin.
The preacher is silent for a few seconds and you assume he (or she) is
having a word of prayer. There's silence for a few more seconds, and
you think he may be gathering his thoughts. Yet when the silence
lasts for around a minute, you start wondering whether something is
wrong and if the preacher is alright.

Silence when there should not be silence is odd, problematic and
questioned.

In contemplation, silence is good and it is to be welcomed in
many other contexts too. We all like peace to concentrate on our
work. We call our personal devotions in the morning, the day time or
the evening a quiet time to indicate the importance of silence. We are
often asked to meditate, pray or remain silent when we enter into the
presence of God. In all these instances, silence is regarded as good. It
is associated with discipline and order. The Bible talks about speaking
less, and how it is better to be silent than to talk foolishly. We read a
lot about this in the Book of Proverbs.

Silence is a problem, however, when a word is needed or an act
is called for. In global political terms, we often come across phrases
such as 'maintaining a studied silence', a 'stubborn silence' or a 'stoic
silence' to describe people in powerful positions who may well be able
to alleviate the problems of a nation or community. When vulnerable
groups are annihilated through war, genocide, displacement and
other similar forces, the world often remains silent. Being critical
of such silence has become one of the essential acts of resistance
movements.

Silence is thus both a good thing, beneficial in many contexts,
and a bad thing if it is resorted to unhelpfully. In the context of
conflict, hate and violence, silence is not neutral. It may seem to
suggest not becoming involved, but maintaining silence does not
mean maintaining innocence. One needs to be active to be silent.
In the context of conflict and broken relationships, silence is a voice,
a perspective, an approach. The Bible says we must not pretend to

41

know nothing and stand by when we need to rescue those who are being led away to death (Proverbs 24.11).

Jesus was concerned with sinners being reconciled with God and with reconciliation between those who were divided in his society. However, in spite of Jesus' invitation, the Jewish leaders found it difficult to reconcile with him or with the common people, who were quite often the victims of their laws, practices and attitudes. One way in which they frequently reacted to what Jesus was doing was to stay silent – a response which is in itself an action.

Throughout his life and ministry, Jesus was always angry when silence blocked his efforts to mend relationships. The Sabbath healings were particularly important in this regard. Although these presented Jesus as a controversial figure to the Pharisees, Scribes and the other elites around him, Jesus' ultimate aim in healing was to aid the marginalized – those who were lepers, blind, diseased or Gentiles – to establish proper relationships with these very elites. Yet he was always opposed, and the silence of those who could have reached out was often a factor in reconciliation failing to take place.

In Luke 14.1–6, we read of Jesus healing a man who had dropsy on the Sabbath. In this story, the Pharisees and lawyers are silent when Jesus asks the question: 'Is it lawful to cure people on the Sabbath or not?'

As the Gospels reveal, instances of Jewish leaders being silent, trying to silence Jesus or being silenced by Jesus occur repeatedly during his ministry. The Jewish leaders often try to test Jesus or to counter his words and actions, but are finally silenced because they are simply unable to answer what Jesus asks.

In this narrative, however, the silence of the Pharisees and lawyers was intentional. Jesus' question was challenging and intended to prove a point – that healing on the Sabbath was not wrong. The Pharisees and lawyers could have responded to this – the fact that they did not means that their silence is deliberate, purposeful and savage, because it is a direct assault on what Jesus is doing. It ignores the difficulties of the man with dropsy and the broader needs Jesus wants to meet in his ministry. It shuns the welfare and healing of a community and the Kingdom values that Jesus was establishing.

The silence of the Pharisees and lawyers also reveals their stubborn hearts. It is not simply that they do not want Jesus to heal this man; they are unwilling to learn from Jesus as to how important it is to help those who are in need. There are relationships in this society that have been lost for centuries and could be rebuilt, but here, the third time a Sabbath healing takes place according to Luke, there is still no change in the attitudes of the Jewish leaders. When Jesus previously healed a man with a withered hand (Luke 6.6–11) and a woman with a spirit that had crippled her for 18 years (Luke 13.10–17), he clearly said and showed the Pharisees and lawyers what should be done. Yet they are unwilling to break their silence.

The silence of the Pharisees and lawyers is not only savage and stubborn, it is also selfish. Jesus points this out when he responds to them with a question in verse 5: 'If one of you has a child or an ox that has fallen into a well, will you not immediately pull it out on a Sabbath day?' This time the Pharisees and lawyers cannot reply because the obvious answer to the question is yes. Jesus is contrasting the selfishness of their silence and how it impacts others with their concern and interest in their own well-being.

In daily life, we see that silence is often kept for selfish reasons. If our self-interest is not served by speaking out, we may well decide against doing so (on the other hand, we may speak or act if that would be beneficial). Jesus challenges this attitude.

In many countries, when communal violence erupts, police and government officials are asked to be silent in order to serve the interests of politicians and others in power. As we read in the stories of this kind of unrest though, silence – even in a small measure by a single official – can harm individuals, families and communities for generations. The selfishness of a few can lead to starvation, displacement and death for many others.

A selfish silence reveals an ignorance, a (willed) lack of understanding of others. The popular Indian writer Arundhati Roy calls such silence a 'project of unseeing'. Silence as a project of unseeing! In the story of Esther in the Bible, Mordecai warns against this kind of unseeing and silence when Esther hesitates to speak to the king about saving the lives of Jews. Mordecai says to Esther: 'If you keep silence at such a time as this, relief and deliverance will rise for the Jews from another quarter but you and your father's family will perish.' (Esther 4.14). Here we see that selfish silence will lead to the destruction of one's own life, although it will never hinder God's ways of acting. Yet when selfish silence is changed into action, it helps the whole community.

The silence of the Pharisees and lawyers, and their failure to answer Jesus' question, indicates that they are unwilling to participate in Jesus' ministry. Perhaps they feel it is beneath them to identify with a man with dropsy? Their silence reflects the private world they are trying to maintain.

Our silence may also sometimes indicate a tendency to isolate ourselves and an unwillingness to respond to Jesus. The call to serve the welfare of others – which will benefit us all – requires that we break silence and answer with our actions.

Breaking silence helps us participate in our community and in the collective effort of building this up. It helps us forge relationships in the context of conflict and violence. Breaking silence is responsible and responsive. The famous poem of Pastor Martin Niemoller, who opposed Hitler's holocaust, goes like this:

> First they came for the Socialists, and I did not speak out—
> Because I was not a Socialist.
> Then they came for the Trade Unionists, and I did not speak out—
> Because I was not a Trade Unionist.
> Then they came for the Jews, and I did not speak out—
> Because I was not a Jew.
> Then they came for me—and there was no one left to speak for me.

We read in the first verse of the Gospel of John that 'In the beginning was the Word', and the verses that follow say that within this Word was light and life for others. The very beingness of the Word and the becoming human of the Word for our salvation indicates the presence of action and participation. This Word, Jesus our Lord, is the Word that is not stubborn, but compassionate and life-giving; it is the Word that is not selfish, but has given everything for others; it is the Word that does not dissociate itself from the world and us, but is dynamic and actively participates in our lives. This is the Word of action. This is the Word that broke its silence in order to re-build the broken relationship between God and us. This is the Word that broke silence to give a voice to the vulnerable. This is the Word that broke silence to challenge us all to break our silence.

Questions for reflection

1 How do we use our silence with regard to the well-being of others?
2 How does silence help and affect the ministry of reconciliation?

3 Are we stubborn in maintaining silence in spite of knowing that we have to act? Are we selfish in maintaining silence because our self-interests are not served? Are we using silence to isolate ourselves from others whom we think are different from us?

10 Rushing to judge

The prayers of the Pharisee and the tax collector

We often hear the story of the Pharisee and the tax collector, a parable, Jesus himself says, for those 'who trusted in themselves that they were righteous and regarded others with contempt' (verse 9). By the end, we are quite clear how important a part humility plays in being acceptable to God.

Yet this story is also about broken relationships. It speaks not only of conceit and self-importance, but of relationships that are not healed. The Pharisee's prayer is a failed attempt at reconciliation with God, and he is supremely unwilling to build a bond with his neighbour, who is right there with him in the temple of God. Instead, the Pharisee rushes to judge. Being judgemental is a serious impediment to restoring broken relationships and building new ones, and a big obstruction to reconciliation.

What is the purpose of going into the presence of God to pray? It is not simply to tell God all we want, but to reconcile with God. Praying to God involves relating to God. It offers us time to reflect on and examine our relationship with God and to set things right. Our worship, liturgy and songs all aim to help us in this.

The Pharisee is not reconciled with God. He is not justified. He is not made righteous. His broken relationship with God is not mended. Why? Because his prayer reveals a critical, condemnatory attitude. Being arrogant and judgemental towards others always go together.

First, the Pharisee judges his neighbour. His words 'like this tax collector' obviously show that they are praying in the temple at the same time. The Pharisee might have joined the tax collector in prayer, which would surely have been pleasing to God, but he is not interested in reconciling with his fellow prayer partner. He goes to the temple to pray, not to engage with others. The phrase 'standing by himself' (verse 11) is important here. He has come to pray, to reconcile with God, yet he wants to be alone. He considers himself unrelated to others, even in the temple of God, even during a time of prayer.

Second, he compares himself with others. He says, 'God, I thank you that I am not like other people: thieves, rogues, adulterers, or even like this tax collector'. He contrasts his perceived righteousness with the perceived unrighteousness of the tax collector, whom he indirectly indicates is not worthy of coming into the presence of God. Seeing ourselves in a dominant position to others is a serious impediment to reconciliation.

Third, he attacks the tax collector, implying that the tax collector should not be there. He is seriously unhappy about this. He demeans the tax collector and his judgemental attitude is unacceptable in the sight of God. As a result, the Pharisee's reconciliation with God fails.

The tax collector, on the other hand, does not compare himself with anyone. He just stands there repentantly, not even looking up to heaven (verse 13).

We all behave like the Pharisee quite often. We like to think of ourselves as unique and special, and the only way we can maintain this fantasy is by regarding others as inferior. We do this both consciously and unconsciously, but this attitude is detrimental to maintaining our relationships with God and our fellow human beings. It is not at all helpful for reconciliation.

Fourth, the Pharisee fails to reconcile with God not only because of the way in which he dismisses others, but because he thinks God will be as judgemental as he. He imagines that God concurs in the Pharisee's high opinion of himself and is unaccepting of thieves, rogues, adulterers and tax collectors. He thinks that God justifies him on account of his fasting and tithes – although, as a learned man, he would certainly be aware of God's words about despising fasting and tithes when humility and justice are not found (Isaiah 58.4–7; Amos 5.21–24; Luke 11.42).

On the other hand, the tax collector *believes* in God's grace, and only in God's grace. He is not bothered about comparing himself with others, but his faith in God's grace indicates that he sees God being gracious to everyone.

In our everyday life, we often make wrong judgements about God and God's dealing with others. Sometimes, we think God will discipline people if they speak against us. I have seen this problem quite often in local church contexts when someone says in the middle of a disagreement, 'God will punish you for speaking against God's person (that's me!)'. This is an error. Our God of grace, as the tax collector affirms, is kind to everyone.

Fifth, the Pharisee fails to reconcile with God because he judges himself wrongly. He has a high opinion of himself. He talks a lot about himself – about what *he is* and what *he is not*; about what he *has* and what he has been *doing* to God (*thinks* he has been doing!) He says, 'I fast twice a week; I give a tenth of all my income' (verse 12). He utters not a single word about what he *lacks* or what he *needs* in order to be reconciled with God.

On the contrary, the tax collector knows himself. He is a sinner. He gets his judgement right, and so becomes acceptable to God and is reconciled with God.

We may not behave or act like the Pharisee in our prayers (although we need to watch ourselves at other times). To pray is not to affirm what I have, what I do and what I can do. It is about what I do not have, what I do not do and what I cannot do. The Pharisee completely misses the point.

This parable also tells us that our understating of self will strongly impact our work of reconciliation. A superior view of one's self compared to others often leads to disconnection, isolation and exclusivism. Being judgemental, making unfavourable comparisons and lacking humility are all serious impediments to reconciliation with God and with others. They will never heal broken relationships, but thinking about what we lack, and believing in God's grace for all, will lead us to mending broken relationships with God and with one another, and to building new relationships with those who are different from us.

Questions for reflection

1 How may judgemental attitudes towards others be affecting our reconciliation with God and with one another?
2 Do we believe God's grace is available for all?
3 How can we make our prayer time one of reconciliation with God and with our fellow human beings?

11 Revenge after reconciliation!

Key text: 2 Samuel 16.5–13, 19.18–23; 1 Kings 2.8–9
David and Shimei

What is false reconciliation? How often do we come across it in our lives? The seeming resolution between David and Shimei in the Old Testament is a classic instance of false reconciliation. It is a story of revenge.

1 The background of Shimei cursing David

Shimei, a Benjaminite (of the same tribe as Saul) curses David as he flees David's son, Absalom. Shimei seems to be a Saul supporter. Although cursing the king (i.e. David) is wrong and one may be punished for it, if we regard what happened between Saul and David as a political power struggle, Shimei may have a point. He is unhappy about the death of Saul and the deteriorating fortunes of Saul's family and holds David accountable, shouting and cursing at him:

> Out! Out! Murderer! Scoundrel! The Lord has avenged on all of you the blood of the house of Saul, in whose place you have reigned; and the Lord has given the kingdom into the hand of your son Absalom. See, disaster has overtaken you; for you are a man of blood.
>
> (2 Samuel 16.7–8)

David's attitude towards and treatment of Saul and his family are not a secret. There is a political war going on and David wants Saul's family and supporters eliminated, lest they pose a threat to his and his descendants' rule.

However, David tries to convince the people several times that he was kind to Saul's family. He kills the young man who 'helped Saul die' (2 Samuel 1.13–16); he kills those who slaughtered Saul's son Ishbaal (2 Samuel 4.9–12) and he demonstrates to the Israelites that he was not responsible for the death of Abner, Saul's commander (2 Samuel 3.36–38). David claims he had a chance to kill Saul more than once, but did not take it (1 Samuel 24.3–7; 26.5–20). Because of the covenant between him and Jonathan, David gets Jonathan's son Mephibosheth (whose feet are crippled and who may not pose much of a threat) to eat with him at his table. Yet we must weigh these positive actions against David's continuing war with Saul's family (2 Samuel 3.1), the fact that he has had several sons of Saul killed (2 Samuel 21.7–9), and that he may have made sure that Saul's daughter Michal bore no children (2 Samuel 6.20–23).

These things – and of course the death of Saul – would definitely have had an impact on the Benjaminites and Shimei may well have disliked David. If Saul were considered a king who usurped the place of God, the judges and the prophets to rule Israel (remember, neither God nor Samuel were happy when people asked for a king (1 Samuel 8.6–8), Shimei sees David as a usurper of Saul's kingdom.

Shimei says to David 'you are a man of blood' (verse 8). In fact, this is true. God calls him a warrior who has shed blood when David tries to build the temple for God (1 Chronicles 28.3).

Of course, in his current situation – fleeing his own son – Shimei's words are certainly not what the king wants to hear.

2 Shimei's reconciliation with David

After Absalom is killed, David is returning to the kingdom when Shimei comes and asks pardon for cursing him. He says to David:

> May my lord not hold me guilty or remember how your servant did wrong on the day my lord the king left Jerusalem; may the king not bear it in mind. For your servant knows that I have sinned; therefore, see, I have come this day, the first of all the house of Joseph to come down to meet my lord the king. (2 Samuel 19.19–20)

Shimei accepts what he did was wrong. He asks for forgiveness. Of course, with David returning to the kingdom and Absalom gone, Shimei realizes he is in deep trouble. We do not know how genuine this apology may be! What we do see here is him meeting with David, acknowledging that he is the first to come in the entire house of Joseph, and unambiguously asking for forgiveness for what he did earlier.

3 David's attitudes to Shimei in public

On both occasions – when Shimei curses David, and later when he comes to ask for forgiveness – David's soldiers want to kill him. David does not allow this. In fact, he expresses no anger towards Shimei at all. The first time he says to his soldiers:

> What have I to do with you, you sons of Zeruiah? If he is cursing because the Lord has said to him, 'Curse David,' who then shall

say, 'Why have you done so?" David said to Abishai and to all his
servants, 'My own son seeks my life; how much more now may this
Benjaminite! Let him alone, and let him curse; for the Lord has
bidden him. It may be that the Lord will look on my distress, and the
Lord will repay me with good for this cursing of me today.

(2 Samuel 16.10–12)

David brings God into the scene and declares publicly that God has
asked Shimei to curse him. Who then should stop him? David also
says that God might change the curse into a blessing. Indeed, God
does so, with David soon reclaiming his kingdom.

David seems to have expected the remnants of the family of Saul
to behave aggressively towards him. This is conveyed clearly when
he speaks of even his son wanting to kill him, so how much more a
person from the tribe of Benjamin? David clearly recognizes this as a
political battle.

The second time Shimei meets David and asks for forgiveness,
David's words 'Shall anyone be put to death in Israel this day? For do
I not know that I am this day king over Israel?' show generosity and
forgiveness. On this joyful occasion, he does not want anyone to be
killed.

David accepts Shimei's confession and promises him in public,
in the name of the Lord (1 Kings 2.8), that he will not die. There is
reconciliation after forgiveness.

4 Revenge after reconciliation

However, David becomes a man involved in false reconciliation. On
his death bed, he clearly instructs Solomon to kill Shimei.

There is also with you Shimei son of Gera, the Benjaminite from
Bahurim, who cursed me with a terrible curse on the day when
I went to Mahanaim; but when he came down to meet me at the
Jordan, I swore to him by the LORD, 'I will not put you to death with
the sword.' Therefore do not hold him guiltless, for you are a wise
man; you will know what you ought to do to him, and you must bring
his grey head down with blood to Sheol. (1 Kings 2.8–9)

Perhaps because he is a Benjaminite, David would expect Shimei to be
a problem for Solomon's kingdom in some way. He might be plotting
tactically, but in responding to the curse of Shimei and in forgiving
Shimei, David quite often uses the Lord's name. It would appear

that this does not mean a great deal to David. Shimei's cursing was allowed by God who turned it into blessing, but now it is 'a terrible cursing' (verse 8). Despite granting Shimei forgiveness and assuring him that he would not die, David has nurtured feelings of vengeance.

From a political point of view you might say this was justified, but in the end, David acts as a hypocrite and covenant breaker, who has made only a false reconciliation – a false reconciliation in the name of the Lord!

Today, we see many political parties and governments, nationally and internationally, making public statements about working together, but doing everything they can to demonize and destabilize one another. This is quite routine and is justified in the name of diplomacy and national security, but can we allow it to happen in Christian life? When we reconcile with God and are assured of forgiveness, how terrible would our lives be if God were still to punish us?

Questions for reflection

1 How often do we reconcile falsely, showing bonhomie on the surface while having hatred in our hearts?
2 What can you honestly do when someone has reconciled with you and you have reconciled with them, yet you feel you have not fully forgiven?
3 Why do you think David really could not forgive Shimei?

12 When someone says sorry

Key text: Jonah 3–4
God, Jonah and the people of Nineveh

'I'm sorry.'

'What do you mean, sorry? . . . You shouldn't have . . .'

This kind of conversation is part of life. We may, on different occasions, be speaker 1 or speaker 2. Speaker 2 is definitely not happy with the apology offered and feels something more is required.

In personal and community life, we often come across two main issues when an effort at reconciliation is made. It may be that a person who has reconciled with us continually makes the same mistake. We get agitated and wonder if we should repeatedly forgive them and be reconciled. (Although, sometimes we may find ourselves in the other person's position and they find themselves in ours!) Jesus' response to Peter on forgiveness (Mathew 18.21–22) offers a clear answer, although it is not at all easy for us to follow. The second issue is that, even when someone is genuinely willing to reconcile with us, or indeed has reconciled with us, we do not find that easy to accept. We would prefer to see the person punished. We want to drag things on rather than settle. Jonah found himself in this position.

Jonah wishes the people of Nineveh to be punished, in spite of the fact that they have confessed their sins, turned from their evil ways and reconciled with God. He finds himself in a situation where he is unable to accept that God has forgiven them. Some suggest Jonah holds this adamant position because of the way in which Nineveh treated Judah and Israel. Although he may loathe Nineveh, as a prophet of God, Jonah must simply rise above his likes and dislikes. This he is unable to do.

We see the people of Nineveh clearly reconciling with God. They make genuine efforts with confession. Even the king of Nineveh rises from his throne, removes his robe, covers himself with sackcloth and sits in ashes (Jonah 3.6). The people have confessed their sins, humbled themselves before God and turned from their evil ways (verse 10).

But Jonah is angry (Jonah 4.1); and he is angry for all the wrong reasons.

Has God changed? Even though the story says that God has relented, God's fundamental nature is the same. God will always forgive and accept anyone who repents and changes their ways (Isaiah 30.18). Of course, Jonah may be thinking that his prophecy would be deemed false if Nineveh is not destroyed. His prophetic work might be at stake. Yet prophetic work is primarily about salvation. It involves destruction only when people do not turn from their evil ways. Jonah should actually be happy that the people of Nineveh have turned to God and that God now has no need to destroy them. His prophetic message has served its purpose well.

However, Jonah finds himself arguing bitterly with God (4.2–3) for forgiving the people of Nineveh. In fact, he acknowledges that God is gracious and merciful, slow to anger, and abounding in steadfast love and ready to relent from punishing (4.2), but he is unable to accept such behaviour from God towards the people of Nineveh. He argues with God for forgiving them. God tries to teach him a lesson by appointing a bush to provide Jonah with shade, only to remove the bush the next day (4.6–7), but Jonah does not relent and keeps arguing. He would have more of a case if God had not spared the people of Nineveh in spite of their confession. His quarrel with God is because God has not destroyed Nineveh, but rather accepted the people's confession and granted forgiveness. Jonah's prophetic message has been a medium for this conversion; he should thank God for making him a channel!

Instead, Jonah waits to see the destruction of Nineveh. He hopes it may be destroyed. He wants to see what will happen to the people (4.5). Unfortunately, Jonah's story becomes the story of a prophet insisting on punishment from God in spite of people repenting, turning from their ways and being forgiven them. Jonah's 'waiting to see' the punishment here is really foolishness. He becomes a classic example of 'even if God gives a blessing, the priest should confirm it'. Instead of waiting outside the city, Jonah should be going to the people and encouraging them to continue to live faithfully.

We all sometimes act like Jonah. Even after people have turned away from their foolish or evil ways, been forgiven by God and reconciled with God and with us, we are unable to overcome feelings of bitterness. We learn that Jonah never felt sorry for what he did. We often find ourselves in a similar position. We think that God will and should punish people we perceive to be God's enemies, often because they are our enemies too. And when God doesn't do that, we get frustrated.

More destructively, we want people to suffer in spite of confessing their mistakes. We convince ourselves their confession is not true and doubt the genuineness of their repentance. Conversely, we might have been involved in saying sorry for something ourselves and finding our neighbours, like Jonah, don't accept our apology. They just keep talking about our mistakes.

Certainly, there are reconciliation acts when it would not be sufficient to say a simple sorry, as that would be a denial of justice if someone has done a wrong and got away with it. Yet there are times when we find ourselves dragging our heels. Despite knowing there is genuine repentance, we may behave like Jonah, which is not at all helpful.

As we carry out the ministry of reconciliation in our Christian life, we often come across problems like these. We need to try to stay open when someone is trying to reconcile with us.

Questions for reflection

1   In what ways might we overcome our personal dislike of someone, and seek God's compassion and mercy for them?
2   How do you feel when someone whom you consider an enemy is forgiven by your friends or by God?
3   How can we overcome the attitude that we may have sometimes of wanting to see someone suffer and be punished?

4

Risking the self

A unique aspect of the Christian ministry of reconciliation is that it invites us to work for the resolution of conflict between others. In general, our involvement in reconciliation is personal: we clash with another person or group, make an effort to sort things out, and so become one of the beneficiaries of the reconciliation process. However, when we look at the ministry of reconciliation undertaken by Jesus Christ in the world, we see that his focus was on reconciling human beings with God and with one another. Jesus was not concerned with personal benefit to himself at all.

In his reconciliation work, Jesus shows solidarity with the vulnerable as well as mediating for them. He was not concerned to point out people's mistakes, and insist they recognize these, before calling them to be reconciled with others. Instead, Jesus makes it clear that in reconciliation someone needs to speak up for those who are actually suffering because of conflict or broken relationships.

Working for reconciliation among others is not easy. It involves taking risks. It means being ready to sacrifice ourselves and what we have for the sake of good relationships between people who may be completely different from us. It means making ourselves vulnerable, being thrown into uncertainty and having the courage to see things through. Working for reconciliation on behalf of the disadvantaged in a conflict is very demanding; in many cases, it will require us to speak to the powerful and plead for the vulnerable.

What risks did Jesus take? He surrendered his very life, facing shame, rejection and the cross. What benefit did Jesus expect? None! How did he bring about reconciliation? By showing solidarity with, and speaking for, those who were vulnerable and persecuted, particularly by those in power.

In this chapter, we look at some characters in the Bible who took risks and were willing to sacrifice their lives, or what they had, in order to spare vulnerable people involved in conflict or broken relationships.

In fact, their efforts did not always result in reconciliation, but we can learn from their willingness to become involved and from their courage. They offer insights and models for our participation in the ministry of reconciliation today:

- Judah risks his life for Benjamin in the context of a conflict between Joseph (the lord of Egypt) and his brothers.
- Moses pleads to God to forgive the Israelites when they are in conflict with God, who is angry and wants to destroy them. Moses prays that his name may be blotted out of God's book if God will not forgive their sins.
- Paul risks his friendship with Philemon, showing solidarity with Onesimus, and is willing to sacrifice what he has to reconcile the two men.
- An unnamed little girl, who is a prisoner in an alien land, risks her life when she asks Naaman to go to the prophet Elisha to be healed from his leprosy.
- Esther risks her life to save her people from the order of Ahasuerus.
- Jonathan risks his life and sacrifices the kingdom due to him in order to make reconciliation between Saul and David – even though this cannot come about.

Above all, Jesus submits his will – which is giving up everything we have – to reconcile us with God and with one another.

13 'Let your servant remain as a slave!'

Key text: Genesis 44.18–34
Judah taking the risk for Benjamin

Although men like Abraham and David were of great importance, the name most used in connection with the identity of the Israelites after they settled in the Promised Land is Judah. Jesus was known as the Son of David, but he was more frequently called the King of the Jews or King of Judah. Why? There are historical reasons for this (such as the northern kingdom being called Israel and the southern kingdom Judah when the country divided after the time of Solomon), but I tend to see some common features between Judah and Jesus. Most importantly, they both pleaded for, and were willing to sacrifice their own lives for an other.

The words of Judah to Joseph in Genesis 44.18–34 are powerful and moving indeed. Personally, this is one of my favourite texts in the Bible, and I return to it again and again.

The background to the story is this. Joseph is sold into slavery by his brothers. They actually want to kill him, but Judah makes a good case for handing him over instead to the Ishmaelites who take him to Egypt (Genesis 37.26–27). Joseph is put in prison when he refuses the advances his master's wife makes towards him. From prison he is taken to the Pharaoh, and when Joseph correctly interprets a dream the Pharaoh has had, he is raised to a position next only to the Pharaoh himself, to rule over the whole of Egypt. Later, when there is a famine, his brothers come to Egypt in search of food and Joseph acts very harshly towards them. He asks them to bring Benjamin, his own brother, born of his mother Rachel. The brothers do so, but when Joseph sends them off with food, he puts his silver cup in Benjamin's sack. Then he instructs his servant to bring the brothers back so that Benjamin can be enslaved. Perhaps Joseph wanted Benjamin with him, but Judah's moving words, pleading for Benjamin and for Jacob, the brothers' father, who would be heartbroken to lose a second son of Rachel, change the course of events. Ultimately, Benjamin and Jacob are saved, and Joseph and his brothers are finally reconciled.

When we look at the life of Judah, we might think that he was not the best of the sons of Jacob. Although Judah did not want Joseph to be killed, he was part of the plan to separate him from the family and particularly from the father who loved him dearly. As a result, Joseph was sold into Egypt as a slave. Judah was also part of the plot to inform Jacob that Joseph was dead, leading Jacob to conclude that Joseph might have been killed by a wild animal (Genesis 37.31–33). Judah keeps silence and lets his father mourn the death of his favourite son. He does not tell the truth.

Then Judah marries a Canaanite woman and becomes the father of sons who were miserable in the sight of the Lord. Later, he tries to deceive his daughter-in-law Tamar by not giving his youngest son to her in marriage when, according to custom, it was his duty to do. Judah even tries to kill Tamar when she takes steps to claim her right (Genesis 38).

Yet, in spite of his misdeeds, Judah is growing in maturity, particularly in his understanding of the pain of others. Even though he does not like Joseph, he does not want him dead; he quickly realizes his mistake in dealing with Tamar and admits this without any fuss (see study 23); and when Jacob is hesitating over sending Benjamin with his brothers to Egypt for food, Judah stresses to his father the importance of living rather than dying, and promises Benjamin's safe return. He says he is accountable to Jacob for Benjamin and if he fails to bring him back, he will bear the blame for ever (Genesis 43.8–10).

These concerns are all reflected in one way or another in Judah's plea to Joseph for Benjamin. Judah is now acting as a responsible person who has given an assurance to his father and wants to live up to it. His words are full of concern for others, unambiguously expressing how difficult he finds it to cope with their pain. He refuses to countenance how devastating it would be to his father to lose Benjamin to suffer slavery in Egypt (verse 34): he says, 'For how can I go back to my father if the boy is not with me? I fear to see the suffering that would come upon my father.' Judah does not want his father to die. Earlier he failed to see the bond between Jacob and Joseph, but now he respects his father's love for Benjamin and affirms how his life is bound up in that of his son (verses 21–22, 30).

Then Judah pleads to Joseph that he will be a slave in place of Benjamin. What would this mean for Judah? What would he have to lose? It appears as if he is risking his entire life.

The possible consequences are these. First, Judah might be punished for speaking to the second most powerful person in the whole of Egypt, someone who is like a Pharaoh, as Judah himself admits (verse 18). It would take a lot of courage for Judah to utter these words. Whatever might happen to Benjamin, Judah could be punished for daring to address Joseph at such length. However, his concern for Benjamin and his father prompt him to do so: he is not speaking for himself.

Second, taking the place of Benjamin as a slave, Judah would be cut off, not only from his father, but also from his own family – his son, daughter-in-law and his grandchildren. He would lose his land, his tribe and his community. As a slave, he would lose his freedom; he would lose everything.

Yet Judah is undeterred. He speaks courageously and passionately to save Benjamin and his father.

It is Judah's powerful and moving words that ultimately make the reconciliation between Joseph and his brothers possible. When he completes his speech, 'Then Joseph could no longer control himself before all those who stood by him, and he cried out, "Send everyone away from me."' (Gen 45.1), Judah's words are so powerful and heartfelt that Joseph cannot control his emotions: 'And he wept so loudly that the Egyptians heard it, and the household of Pharaoh heard it' (verse 2).

Joseph has been very tough with his brothers for years. He even imprisoned Simeon when the others returned to Canaan to fetch Benjamin, but although Joseph has undoubtedly suffered at his brothers' hands, he cannot control himself when Judah takes the great risk of speaking up to him, and offering himself as a slave in place of Benjamin.

We quite often credit Joseph for his generosity and willingness to reconcile with the brothers who have acted with great evil towards him. We do so rightly, but we cannot overlook the role played by Judah and the powerful plea he made, risking all he had. If the question arises as to why Jesus was born of the tribe of Judah rather than of the other eleven tribes, perhaps this text has an answer. Here we see Judah doing the work Jesus will later do – offering himself as a sacrifice in the place of others so that they might have life.

Questions for reflection

1 How often are we conscious of feeling the pain of others?
2 What we can learn from Judah's life? How might we plead for others?

3 Judah refuses to countenance the suffering of his father and brother and would rather suffer himself. What spurs us on when we know we have to work for reconciliation between others so that the vulnerable in the conflict are protected?

14 'Blot me out of the book that you have written!'

Key text: Exodus 32

Moses is willing to sacrifice his life to reconcile the Israelites with God

The Israelites are on the way from Egypt to the Promised Land and Moses is leading them. When they arrive at Mount Sinai, Moses goes to speak with God on the mountain and he receives from God the tablets containing God's commandments. Before he returns to his people, the Israelites sin against God and make a golden calf to worship as a god. God is very angry and wants to destroy the Israelites, but Moses pleads for them.

Moses' prayer to God to forgive the Israelites, and his willingness to have his name 'blotted out from the book God has written' if God will not forgive them, is an example of someone risking his own life for the sake of reconciliation between two others. What lessons can we learn from Moses for our ministry of reconciliation today?

1 Moses pleads to God in spite of many odd factors

The first odd thing is that the Israelites have always been rebellious. When they were still in Egypt and God sent Moses to redeem them from the hands of Pharaoh, they murmured against Moses and Aaron (Exodus 5.20–22). In the wilderness they quite often murmur against Moses, Aaron and God – when they are between the Red Sea and the armies of Egypt (Exodus 14.10–12); when they don't have water to drink or only water that is bitter (15.24, 17.2–3); when they want food (16.2–3), and on several subsequent occasions. At one point, their rebelliousness is so great that Moses asks God to kill him. He says:

> Why have you treated your servant so badly? Why have I not found favour in your sight, that you lay the burden of all this people on me? Did I conceive all this people? Did I give birth to them, that you should say to me, 'Carry them in your bosom, as a nurse carries a sucking child, to the land that you promised on oath to their ancestors'? . . . I am not able to carry all this people alone, for they are too heavy for me. If this is the way you are going to treat me, put me to death at once – if I have found favour in your sight – and do not let me see my misery. (Numbers 11.11–15)

However, it is very interesting that here on Mount Sinai we see Moses as a person who has developed an affection for the people he has been leading, in spite of their insubordination. Here he is even willing to give his life for these recalcitrant souls. He pleads to God for people who have repeatedly proven themselves problematic in the eyes of Moses and in the eyes of God.

Second, God has already made an 'offer' to Moses – that God will make of him a great nation (Exodus 32.10). It is important that this really tempting offer comes before Moses submits his plea to God. Moses has something great in prospect, but the promise of blessing from God does not turn his head. He cannot behave selfishly and leave the Israelites to be burned by God's anger, however much they rebel. Perhaps Moses sees his blessing as very much tied up with the Israelites being blessed by God. He cannot think about his welfare without thinking about theirs. Moses is an example of someone not persuaded by God's assurance of personal blessing if such blessing is not connected with the blessing of a whole people.

2 The interesting conversations between God and Moses

In verse 7, God refers to the Israelites as 'your [Moses'] people whom you brought up out of the land of Egypt.' There is a chilly tone of disowning and distancing here, indicating a broken relationship between God and the Israelites.

However, Moses' response is interesting. He says, 'O LORD, why does your wrath burn hot against *your* people, whom *you* brought out of the land of Egypt with great power and with a mighty hand?' (verse 11). Moses counters that the people are God's, not his. God was responsible for bringing them out of Egypt, not him. Importantly, Moses makes this point by reminding God of God's might and power.

Moses is also concerned that the Gentiles should not speak ill of God by saying that God brought the Israelites out of Egypt simply to kill them on the way to the Promised Land (verse 12). His pleas are based on God's mercy and compassion, and on God's promises to Abraham, Isaac and Israel that God will multiply their descendants.

Moses' words are powerful. Rarely do we come across someone who speaks to God like this. Rarely does someone tell God what to do and what not to do. Moses does not seem to be offering a simple, direct prayer, but a counter-argument! He is arguing against what God wants to do, but God does not get angry with Moses for speaking these words. Instead, God has a change of mind about the planned disaster to befall the Israelites (verse 14).

3 Blot me out of the book that you have written

Moses clearly acknowledges that the people have acted sinfully by making a golden calf as their god, but he asks for forgiveness for them. If God is not willing to forgive them, but will only punish them, he requests that he be punished instead. He asks God to blot out his name from the book God has written, to have his name erased. We might speculate about exactly what this phrase means, but it seems to convey clearly that Moses is willing to sacrifice his life for the sake of God's people. He is ready to die, if that is necessary. In making this offer, Moses does not think about himself. He forgets himself. He is not mindful of offending God.

Given the backstory, Moses' offering to sacrifice his own life for the Israelites is really quite astonishing. First, he didn't want to bring them out of Egypt when God called him to and made all kind of excuses. He has since witnessed their rebelliousness several times and complained to God about this. Yet he knows that they will be vulnerable if God's anger breaks out, and he is willing to speak for them, and ready to give his life for them.

Moses' words remind us that words of mediation are highly necessary in the context of conflict and reconciliation, although he does not simply mediate, but almost *argues* with God. He speaks for the rebellious people, knowing that only God's forgiveness of the Israelites and reconciliation with God will save them. He is not concerned with God's promise to make of him a great nation if the people he is leading will not be part of that blessing.

Of course, the reconciliation Moses is aiming for does not happen fully and immediately. God gets very angry and some people are killed because of their rebelliousness against God. Yet what is important is that, through his pleading and his coming before the presence of God again and again, Moses takes a risk for the Israelites. He is willing to sacrifice everything for them.

Questions for reflection

1 What thoughts dominate our minds when we need to plead with someone who is rebellious and not in a good relationship with us?
2 How often do we pray for those whom we think may not like us?

3 Are we able to enjoy God's blessing in our lives when others in society, for various reasons, are not experiencing well-being? How can we feel blessed alongside those whom we do not like and who may not like us?

15 'If he owes you anything, charge that to my account'

Key text: Philemon
Paul mediating for Onesimus

How do we approach speaking to a friend about forgiving and accepting a person whom we like but our friend does not? Our inclination is likely to be to keep quiet and maintain our relationship with each person. Paul finds himself in a situation where someone he likes is in conflict with another of Paul's friends, but he decides to ask his friend to accept this other person, thereby risking many things, including his relationship with his friend.

Paul's letter to Philemon is unique in many ways. It is a letter written to an individual to support another individual. Although many of Paul's other letters are concerned with reconciliation – between God and human beings, between Jews and Gentiles, among quarrelling Christians in the churches – this letter seeks to promote reconciliation between two individuals: a slave and his owner.

The story is this. Onesimus was a slave of Philemon, but he ran away. We don't know the contributing factors, although Onesimus is unlikely to have taken this action lightly. First century fugitive slaves were heavily punished, often by death. Onesimus happens to meet Paul and is converted to Christ by his preaching. On an earlier occasion, Paul had preached the gospel to Philemon and he is now a Christian too. This is the context in which Paul attempts to reconcile Onesimus and Philemon. Paul is now imprisoned and he thinks that Onesimus might be helpful to him in these circumstances, but he feels more strongly that Onesimus needs to be reconciled with Philemon. The effort of bringing about this reconciliation is considerable, as we read from Paul's letter. He has to plead for Onesimus, taking the side of this vulnerable person who is susceptible to punishment for escaping from his master. He refers to Onesimus as one 'who is my very heart' (verse 12). Paul has to risk his relationship with Philemon, in the process. This Paul is ready to do.

In the letter to Philemon we see a lot of apprehension, something not often evident in Paul's other epistles. He is certainly concerned about how Philemon will regard him favouring the acceptance of a runaway slave. He wonders if Philemon will be happy with the letter, yet he commits to writing it. What are the things he risks? What is he willing to sacrifice for the sake of reconciliation between Philemon and Onesimus, so the former forgives and accepts the latter instead of punishing him for what he has done?

First, Paul risks his relationship with Philemon.

It is clear from the letter that Paul and Philemon enjoy a very good relationship. Paul knows what Philemon does for the apostles and the disciples. He addresses him as friend and co-worker (verse 1). He appreciates his love for the saints (verses 5–7).

The way Paul writes shows that he is concerned his relationship with Philemon should not suffer, although he is afraid that it might because he is, after all, pleading for a run-away slave. In verse 14 Paul says that he will do nothing without Philemon's consent, and in verse 17 he asks him to welcome Onesimus 'if you consider me your partner'. These words are not simply to flatter Philemon, but indicate that Paul is indeed is concerned about their relationship, and that he is taking the risk of sacrificing it.

Rarely do we feel relaxed about forgoing our relationships with the powerful for the sake of others. World politics is indicative of this. Are we willing to take risks for the growing number of migrants and refugees if that will put us in trouble with powerful governments? Are we willing to talk about the poor if that will anger corporate bodies? We often restrain ourselves. We abstain, thinking that silence is neutral. Paul shows that it is not. Taking risks is important even if this involves a deterioration of our relationships with those in power.

Second, Paul is willing to waive his authority.

Even though he is in a position to command Philemon, Paul would rather entreat him. He says, 'I am bold enough in Christ to command', but in fact he appeals (verses 8–9). This demonstrates that Paul is, unusually, not exerting his authority. His is generally quite uncompromising in his letters! In writing to the Corinthian church, he gives a kind of warning, saying 'What would you prefer? Am I to come to you with a stick, or with love in a spirit of gentleness?' (1 Corinthians 4.21). In his letter to Philemon, however, Paul is willing to waive his authority so that Onesimus will be accepted. He is willing to give up his right to command. It is interesting to note that, in spite of saying that he is appealing, Paul's language appears a little commanding: he tells Philemon he is 'confident of your *obedience*' (verse 21). Paul is not being hypocritical here. Rather we see that, although he is in a position to exercise his authority, he would prefer to appeal for the sake of a vulnerable person who needs to be reconciled with his master. He is willing to give up his higher position in order to plead for Onesimus.

Third, Paul is willing to sacrifice what he has.

Paul writes to Philemon that if Onesimus owes him anything (verse 18), it may be charged to Paul. Philemon would have incurred a financial loss in Onesimus running away, and Paul does not want this to affect their reconciliation. He is willing to sacrifice his wealth in order to pay what may be owed, on behalf of Onesimus. The way Paul reassures – 'I, Paul, am writing this with my own hand: I will repay it' (verse 19) – indicates that the sum may be large. Whatever the amount, Paul expresses that he does not want his words to be mere words, but that he really means them.

In Paul, we see an example of someone risking a close relationship with a friend, being willing to waive his authority, and offering to share what he has – for the sake of reconciliation between two unequal people. The Christian ministry of reconciliation is not a comfortable journey where things go smoothly. It is definitely a joy and pleasure when reconciliation comes about, but the process is painful and hazardous. When we undertake to reconcile two unequal people (in that one is more vulnerable), the risks will be particularly high. This is the way Christian reconciliation works.

Questions for reflection

1 Can you recall a time you chose not to speak with a friend on behalf of a more vulnerable friend because you thought your relationship with first would suffer?
2 Are we willing to invest our personal finances in reconciliation work in and between churches?
3 How does it feel when we have to back down from a commanding position for the sake of reconciliation?

16 The courageous little girl

Key text: 2 Kings 5
The healing of Naaman

We are probably all aware of a conflict that might be resolved if we offered some of the resources at our disposal to facilitate reconciliation – or if we spoke or acted in some way. Often we are not much inclined to become involved; we do not want our interests to be affected or our comfort zones to be disturbed. However, in the narrative of 2 Kings, which is regarded as a miracle story, we read of a little girl, with no resources of her own, who risks her life by speaking up. As a result, Naaman, the great commander of the Syrian army, is healed of his leprosy by God's prophet Elisha in Israel, and the little girl effects no less than a connection between two hostile countries.

In ancient Israel, the relationship between Israel and Syria was unsettled. There were wars quite frequently – indeed, if they had not had a war for three years, that was too long! (1 Kings 22.1). The hostility between these two countries meant that the Syrians were often attacking Israel. Hence, for the little girl to suggest to Naaman that he goes for healing to a country with which his is constantly at war is astonishing. She does not let the issues between these two nations stop her from intervening. It would have been wiser if she had kept her mouth shut, but she breaks silence and acts. She takes a huge risk because she has many disadvantages. There are lots of reasons why she might be despised and brushed aside:

- First, she is young. We know that in ancient societies (and still in some today), attitudes to children and young people are often quite negative. Their voices are seldom taken seriously. It is always an adult world.
- She is a girl. The role of women in public life is suppressed to a great extent in ancient Israel (as it is still in many contemporary societies), and they have very little say when it comes to matters concerning rulers or kings.
- She is a slave. We read that she was taken captive from Israel (2 Kings 5.2) and a slave advising her master is quite unimaginable. Perhaps Naaman's wife was fond of her. Nevertheless, it would not be easy for her to make a suggestion regarding her master's health.
- She is a foreigner. She is not Syrian.

- She is not a political person.
- She speaks without being asked to and might have expected to be punished for this. It would take a lot of courage to address her mistress in such a way.

Against these disadvantages, let us consider the advantages of Naaman. He is an adult, a man, a slave master, a mighty warrior who is the military commander for the whole of Syria, and he is one of the top men in the country with access to any king at any time. Moreover, he is quick to anger, easily irritated, dominating (verse 11), and has pride in his own land (verse 12).

Yet, we see that the little girl has the confidence to speak, the courage to ask Naaman to go to another country to be healed, and that she seems sure the prophet in Israel will heal Naaman. Her faith in God and in God's prophet is so high that she risks everything. We may wonder how she knows that God's prophet will heal Naaman. We may think about the 'what if' question: what would have happened to the girl if the prophet had not healed Naaman? Yet she does not consider such questions at all. We have here many wonderful pointers for our ministry of reconciliation. God has a number of ways of connecting hostile countries and bringing about reconciliation between warring people. Working for reconciliation involves believing that God is the author and master of reconciliation and that God guides the process. God is fully involved in our reconciliation efforts; we are not acting alone. God wants people who have been created in the image of God to live together. This little girl teaches us this lesson through her courageous act.

As she crosses boundaries, so does Naaman. His healing is closely connected to his ability to cross not only political, but also many of the social and cultural boundaries of his day.

The narrative of 2 Kings 5 (and 6) does not tell us that the little girl's act brought about complete reconciliation between Israel and Syria. Relations fluctuate again between hostility and hospitality (2 Kings 6.21–23), but she took a risk when she need not have, and unwittingly helped to improve relations between two nations, at least for a while.

Questions for reflection

1 How can we make better use of the opportunities God gives us to bring about reconciliation between others?

2   What does it mean to come out of our comfort zone? What can we learn from this little girl, who was not in any kind of comfort zone at all?

3   In Naaman's story, we see that healing is closely connected to crossing boundaries. Later in the New Testament, Jesus often crosses the boundaries to heal others. Reflect on the connections between crossing boundaries, healing and reconciliation.

17 'If I perish, I perish!'

Key text: Esther 4
Esther takes a risk to save her people

The story of Esther is about how God saves God's people (although God never appears in the book directly) through elevating Esther to the position of queen in the kingdom of Ahasuerus. We read at the beginning of chapter 4 that Mordecai (a Jew, the cousin of Esther and instrumental in her advancement) will not bow down before Haman, the close aide of King Ahasuerus. As a result, Haman requests that the king issue an order that all the Jews are to be destroyed. The only way they may be saved is by someone pleading for them, but going into the presence of the king is a serious problem, even for the queen, because there is a law that no one can do so unless he or she has been summoned. Someone has to risk breaking the law, and it falls to Esther to do so. She goes to the king and, in due course, overturns the order for killing the Jews and saves her people.

We generally see Esther as a heroine, and she is a symbol of courage for many of us – one of the handful of women in the Bible who act boldly to carry out God's plans for God's people. From Esther's point of view, things look quite different. When Mordecai confronts her after she says that she cannot do anything in spite of being the queen, Esther is not lying or indifferent to Mordecai's demands and advice. Rather, we might assume she is paralysed by terror, so she hesitates to go to the king and speak for her people. She knows she has to break the law; she knows she has to risk everything, including her life, to carry this out. When Mordecai warns her harshly (that she cannot escape in spite of being the queen) and persuades her to intervene (verses 13–14), she does not respond directly to his words, but only says:

> Go, gather all the Jews to be found in Susa, and hold a fast on my behalf, and neither eat nor drink for three days, night or day. I and my maids will also fast as you do. After that I will go to the king, though it is against the law; and if I perish, I perish.

The way ahead is not easy. Esther's fear is obvious when she asks Mordecai and others to fast as she prepares to enter the presence of the king. Her anxiety clearly illustrates that she is not doing something simple. She already knows from the fate of her predecessor, Queen Vashti, that the king and his people do not like women standing up to their husbands. When she speaks up herself, what will happen? She is going to have to disclose a fact she has been hiding (as instructed by Mordecai) – that she is Jewish. Esther's words, 'If I perish, I perish' may appear courageous, but they reveal her distress. She is suffering a great deal even as she finally agrees to take risks for her people.

The first risk relates to the fact that Esther's influence is seriously limited.

The order to kill the Jews that Haman has been able to elicit from the king is out everywhere, but it appears Esther is unaware of it. In spite of being a queen and being in the palace, she does not know what is happening around her. We can be certain she is not acting disingenuously when she sends people to ask Mordecai why he is in distress.

Esther's words to Mordecai and the apprehension she shows indicate that, in spite of being a queen, in spite of being the wife of the most powerful person in the empire, she is treated as an ordinary woman in the kingdom. She cannot simply go to her husband. She is in the most powerful place in the country, yet she says, 'if any man or woman goes to the king . . .' (verse 11), which reveals that she thinks of herself as only 'a woman'. For a queen to be treated in this way seems ridiculous, but it makes it clear that Esther's influence is less than we might expect.

The second risk relates to breaking the law. Everyone knows what the law is, and Esther is aware that she could easily be killed if her entry angers the king. She knows what happened to Vashti, who refused to go before the king when asked to do so. Esther's act of going to the king without being invited or summoned may be regarded as even more disrespectful. At least Vashti was only thrown out; Esther could be killed – unless the king is kind.

The third risk she takes is that she may have to give up her life. When we take risks, we have to cope with uncertainty. Esther's 'If I perish, I perish' reflects that she simply cannot foresee what will happen, but in a sense, she does know what she is doing. It is quite clear that she has to make herself vulnerable if the king is to change his attitude towards the Jews.

What does Esther risk? What will she lose if the king does not hold out his golden sceptre?

She will lose the love of her husband.
She will lose her privileges.
She will lose her position as a queen.
She will lose her life.
Yet she decides to risk all these to save her people.

In the end, Esther's story is not one of overt reconciliation: it is about saving the Jews from the hands of Haman. Due to his actions, there is a crisis, with the Jews on one side and the king's people on the other. There must be reconciliation between the king and the Jews if the latter are to be saved, and someone has to make that happen.

As later events show, saving the Jews leads to revenge for the Jews. After taking a huge risk to plead to the king for her people, Esther thinks killing the Jews' enemies is the ultimate way to save them. This is quite the opposite of lessening hate and building relationships. However, the effort Esther took to speak up for her people, at great risk to her well-being and herself, are impressive.

Questions for reflection

1 How do you feel when you know you will have to subvert convention or break the law in order to save someone vulnerable?
2 When did you last enter into a period of uncertainty for the sake of building relationships among others?
3 Do you think Esther is justified, after saving her people from elimination, to seek orders from the king to kill their enemies?

18 A friend who risked himself for his friend

Key text: 1 Samuel 19–20
Jonathan and David

One of the best friendship stories in the Bible is that about Jonathan and David. I think their friendship is next only to that between Jesus and his disciples. Now, it could well be that the story of Jonathan and David was written from a Davidic kingdom perspective to justify the passing of the kingdom from Saul to David. Yet in simple terms, what we see here is Jonathan affirming his friendship with David, and even risking his life to save David from the hands of Saul.

The background is this. When the people become dissatisfied with the rule of the judges, Saul, from the tribe of Benjamin, is elected to be the first king over Israel. That the Israelites have requested a king does not please God (or Samuel, as you may recall!), but God asks Samuel to anoint Saul. Some time later, displeased by Saul's actions, God asks Samuel to anoint David, even though he is very young and has no experience of fighting for his land. Then David kills Goliath – in a victory for the Israelites over the Philistines – and becomes closer to Saul. When David's victory is recognized and celebrated by the people, Saul gets angry and tries to eliminate him. However, Saul's son Jonathan and daughter Michal like David and try to protect him. David and Michal marry each other and Jonathan becomes David's best friend.

Jonathan learns about his father's hatred because David so often has to flee for safety. He realizes he must attempt a Saul-David reconciliation to protect David, although he knows this will involve taking many risks.

1 No one else but David is the threat to the throne of Jonathan

We should note no one other than David is a threat to the kingdom of Jonathan; Jonathan is the legitimate political heir to Saul. He is his eldest son and a mighty warrior who has participated in battles with his father and is loved by all the people. Why should he not be the next ruler?

Obviously Jonathan knows that protecting David will frustrate any personal desire he himself has for the kingdom, which would naturally come to him. Perhaps he thinks David would be a better choice than himself? Saul thinks otherwise. As any king might, Saul sees David as a threat to Jonathan and is angry that Jonathan is not mindful of this (1 Samuel 20.31).

2 No one else but his own father is against David

Jonathan is aware that he will earn the wrath of his father if he supports David (1 Samuel 20.3–34). Yet he takes David's side and makes the most of every opportunity to reconcile him and Saul.

First, on different occasions Jonathan intercedes for David. He puts to Saul that David should not be killed and gives many reasons which seem to convince his father: 'The king should not sin against his servant David, because he has not sinned against you, and because his deeds have been of good service to you; for he took his life in his hand when he attacked the Philistine, and the Lord brought about a great victory for all Israel. You saw it, and rejoiced; why then will you sin against an innocent person by killing David without cause?' (1 Samuel 19.4–5). Saul heeds Jonathan and promises that he will not seek to kill David, but soon he is hunting for him again. Once more, Jonathan intercedes for David when he does not turn up for the new moon feast with the king (1 Samuel 20.30).

Second, when mediation and intercession do not work, Jonathan confronts his father for the sake of his friend. He makes it clear that he disapproves of Saul's plan to kill David, but this angers Saul, who abuses and humiliates Jonathan, saying, 'You son of a perverse, rebellious woman! Do I not know that you have chosen the son of Jesse to your own shame, and to the shame of your mother's nakedness?' (1 Samuel 20.30). Such ugly words from his father are surely an insult to the prince. As well as being disgraced and ridiculed in public, he is accused of spoiling the plans and wishes his father has for him, to say nothing of the risk of losing his love. None of this will stop Jonathan from protecting David.

Third, in addition to facing the anger and abuse of his father, Jonathan comes close to being murdered. When he takes David's side, Saul tries to kill his own son. On the one hand, Jonathan is losing the kingdom to his friend and, on the other, we see him almost losing his life because of his father.

Jonathan informs David about Saul's plans to kill him time and again (1 Samuel 19.1–2; 20.18–23; 35–40). The way in which they make arrangements to meet suggests that Jonathan and David realize Saul has arranged for spies to keep them under constant scrutiny. Meeting David is definitely hazardous, but Jonathan is ready to put his life on the line for his friend.

Jonathan is convinced that reconciliation between David and Saul is vital for David's welfare, and he tries to bring this about through mediation, confrontation and risking his own life. True to his name, Jonathan gives everything for the sake of an other.

Questions for reflection

1 How do you cope when trying to reconcile two other people takes a toll on your physical, mental or spiritual well-being?
2 How would it feel to pray for a friend who needs your help to receive something you want for yourself?
3 Have you ever been in conflict with your own family, friends or community through deciding to speak for the vulnerable?

19 'Not my will, but yours be done!'

Key text: Luke 22.41–42
Submission of will as Jesus' identity

Friedrich Nietzsche, the famous German philosopher, introduced the idea of 'will to power' to describe what he believed may be the main driving force for human beings. He argued that the strong achieve power through pride and dominion, which he called master morality, and the weak achieve it through valuing humility, self-denial and compassion for others, which he called slave morality. In Nietzsche's understanding, Christian morality was slave morality. However, Jesus clearly demonstrated through his own humility, self-denial and compassion that these brought life to others, rather than power to himself. While we cannot deny that Christians have been and are still heavily interested in various kinds of power and dominion over others (which is one of the reasons Nietzsche was highly critical of Christianity), such attitudes are definitely not derived from what Christ did. In fact, I believe the existence and growth of Christianity have depended on those Christians who have witnessed to Christ by submitting their will to God for the sake of others, rather than those who have imposed the faith through power and pride.

'Will to power' seeks power for oneself, but Jesus' submission of his will to God is never to gain power. It is purely for the sake of others, for the purpose of reconciling sinful humanity with God and with one another, so we may all have fullness of life.

'Not my will, but yours be done.' Jesus affirms this when he prays to God in Gethsemane, during the most difficult time of his human life. We can hardly imagine the pain, the agony Jesus is enduring here as a human being. Little wonder he asks God if he can bypass the cross; yet he is willing to submit his will to God's.

What happens in Gethsemane is not that there is a difference between what God wills and what Jesus wills – Jesus already knows God's will and has been doing it all his life. There is not a struggle over whose will might prevail. We might say that God praying to be spared God's will is a mystery of the Trinity.

Not only when he was nearing the cross, but right from the beginning, Jesus was aware that he was on earth to do his Father's will, rather than his own. In John 6.38, he states this unambiguously:

'for I have come down from heaven, not to do my own will, but the will of him who sent me.'

He is always ready to allow God's will to take the place of his own. Not only his death, but Christ's very incarnation is to do with God's will. In becoming incarnate, Christ loses the equal place he has with God (Philippians 2). On another occasion, Jesus tells the people around him, 'Very truly, I tell you, the Son can do nothing on his own, but only what he sees the Father doing; for whatever the Father does, the Son does likewise' (John 5.19).

Jesus' submission involved knowing God's will, and the voluntary way in which he entered into this, is the most important aspect of his submission. Jesus is aware he has every privilege. He knows who he is. We might find it impossible to submit our will if we had every privilege, but it is possible for Christ.

During his entire ministry, Jesus encourages his disciples (and through them us) to affirm that God's will – and God's will alone – be done in heaven and on earth. This features strongly in the prayer he taught (Matthew 6.10).

What is submitting one's will?

Let us imagine a situation in which we are to do someone else's will. Can you imagine how that would feel? Perhaps giving up one's life might be easier. For submitting your will, being constantly reminded that you are here to do as someone else wishes and have no capacity to act on your own, is perhaps the most difficult thing on the earth. It is negating the entire self. Speaking, acting, hearing and doing according to someone's will is self-denial *while living*. It is allowing someone else to control what you do.

Also, submitting one's will is more than mere obedience. We may be obedient for various reasons, even when we do not want to be. For example, we may be compelled to submit our will to protect our interests. Yet in Jesus' submission of his will, we see a wholly voluntary act, and we see wholeness. He submits everything, even though this leads to death on a cross.

Jesus submits his will to God's will for the sake of others

There is an additional wonder to Jesus' submission of his will. It is not simply a matter between him and God, although it appears to be, for there is a third group involved – sinful humanity. Jesus submits his will entirely for the sake of healthy relationships between others.

It becomes eminently clear that, more important than his own pain to Jesus, is that of God and that of God's people, which is caused by alienating ourselves from God. I have often wondered, when fighting discrimination and injustice, how we can remain obsessed with our own pain while completely neglecting the pain felt by others involved. If we want to be free of pain and suffering, that is perfectly understandable, but it will be possible only when others are free of pain too. Jesus' submission of his will is an invitation to take the risk of considering our pain in relation to the pain and suffering of others. At the very least, we should avoid talking about our pain if we are not open to the pain of others. We cannot speak the language of self-defence here.

Submission of one's will is the greatest thing one can do. Jesus submits his will for our sake, to reconcile us with God. He gives the maximum he can offer – his very self in its entirety. He submits his will so that there will be life for others.

In the Old Testament, Haman and Ahitophel are examples of people whose will is closely identified with their entire self, existence and identity. When their will is completely rejected, they would prefer to be dead than to go on living (see Esther 6.12 and 2 Samuel 17.23).

'Not my will but yours' is perhaps the most powerful statement in the history of Christianity. Jesus' entire life and ministry can be summarized in this one phrase. Here is an attitude that makes others central in our life. If the focus on the other vanishes, Christianity loses its relevance and so does the Christian ministry of reconciliation. I often think that, to understand the decline of Christianity today, we need do no more than focus on when, where and how we have lost the centrality of the 'other' in relation to ourselves.

Questions for reflection

1 Do you feel that submitting your will would be more difficult than giving up your life? If so, why and how?
2 Consider the ways in which humility and self-denial are essentially connected with our ministry of reconciliation.
3 Christianity from the beginning is about the other. When

that aspect is lost, Christianity loses its essence. What are your thoughts on this?

5

Humility and self-criticism

A sense of humility and the ability to be self-critical are both essential to building human relationships and in the process of reconciliation. Yet today they are often despised or considered weak and cowardly. In fact, when Christianity began, attitudes were not dissimilar. Greek society valued pride and valour highly and belittled humility. In Aristotelian ethics, the goal of human life was *eudaimonia* (flourishing), achieved by the accumulation of honour and virtue. A strong man had the virtue of being *megalopsychos* ('a great-souled [or proud] man') and a faint-hearted one the vice of being *mikropsychos* ('a small-souled [or humble] man'). The humility taught and practised by Jesus was a direct challenge to this understanding and approach. For God's humbling of God, revealed in Christ coming among us, was an expression of divine grace, and the imitation of this by Christ's followers is essential for Christian discipleship and mission. We owe the early Christian communities much; they transformed humility from a vice into something that became foundational for Christianity, through which we can express care for the other and build healthy relationships with one another.

That humility contributes to well-functioning relationships, and a lack of humility and self-criticism leads to further breakdown in relationships, is our everyday experience. When we are in the process of making up after a conflict, we often rush to claim that we are the victim, while the other person is responsible for what has gone wrong. We shall have to set aside our ego and pride if we are to take the initiative to reconcile with the other. Rediscovering the importance of humility and self-criticism is vital for those committed to carrying out the ministry of reconciliation effectively.

This chapter has seven studies on the need for humility and self-criticism in building relationships and in the reconciliation process.

There are many villains in the stories we read in the Bible, and sometimes we can learn from them too. In fact, we may find ourselves behaving more arrogantly and unrepentantly than they do! We are critical of the scribes and Pharisees who brought the woman caught in adultery to Jesus, yet unlike them, we may refuse to listen to Jesus even when he is telling us to 'let anyone among you without sin be the first to throw a stone'. We discover how a unique saying in the Bible, 'Am I God?', which seems to come out of a self-deprecating attitude in the context of human relationships, is used quite differently. Then there is the lawyer's apparently innocent question to Jesus, 'who is my neighbour?', which actually reveals a lack of humility and a desire for control in knowing and relating to others. Judah (whom we met earlier) quickly realizes and admits he is in the wrong and his daughter-in-law is in the right when there is a crisis in their family. The long-reigning ruler Manasseh spends many years behaving in an evil manner before humbling himself and reconciling with God. The people around Jesus display arrogance, believing that they can see while others cannot, which is a major stumbling block to their reconciliation with Jesus and others in their society.

20 Learning self-criticism from the antagonists

Key text: John 8.1–11
The accusers who related, realized and retracted

Which character do you most identify with when reading John 8.1–11? With the woman who is accused? With Jesus? With the people around him who are looking to see how he will respond? Or with the woman's antagonists, the scribes and Pharisees?

This story is perhaps the most significant narrative we have of Jesus Christ displaying compassion towards sinners during his life on earth. It takes place in the Temple premises where the scribes and the Pharisees bring a woman caught in adultery to Jesus. They ask him to pronounce punishment by way of testing him, hoping he will get caught between the Law of Moses and the law of the Romans. Jesus' powerful words, 'let anyone among you who is without sin be the first one to throw a stone at her' is a challenge to which they are unable to respond, except by taking their leave one by one. Jesus says to the woman, 'Neither do I condemn you. Go your way and from now on do not sin again.'

We may have found ourselves in a similar position to that of the woman caught in adultery – badly thought of by people around us, but waiting in hope for God to act. We appreciate and praise our Lord for offering forgiveness, which gives us confidence that we too have been pardoned for our sins. Yet without any doubt, it is difficult to identify with the 'villains' of the piece, the scribes and Pharisees. Or is it? We tend to take a 'holier than thou' attitude towards these leaders, and can end up thinking we are much better than they. However, these villains, convicted by the words of Jesus, do actually realize that they are sinful and they leave the place without harming the woman or getting into any further argument with Jesus. Do we not behave even more badly when it comes to our attitudes to others? In fact, there is something to be learned from the antagonists, as we now explore.

1 The antagonists relate to the woman they accused

The attitude of the antagonists in the first half of the story clearly implies that they feel quite detached from the woman and her acts; they regard her, not as one amongst them, but as an aberration in their otherwise normal society. This is evident from their actions. They 'bring' her to Jesus, refer to her as 'this woman' and make her stand in front of the crowd. They want to shame her publicly, which may not have been strictly necessary according to Jewish law, but will help them prove a point. The man is notably absent, although Leviticus 20.10 and Deuteronomy 22.22 say that both the man and the woman involved in adultery should be stoned. However, the antagonists carefully tailor their words to speak about 'such women' (verse 5). There is a suggestion that they have nothing to do with this woman or with her sin. They represent the normal; she represents the aberration.

When Jesus speaks, these opponents of his are given no option but to relate to this real woman and consider their sin in the light of hers. Jesus is implying that sin is relational in character. He is not dealing with a collective sin here – clearly it is personal – but even in personal sin, the role of society is crucial. There are at least two things we might consider with regard to the relational character of sin: first, that the scribes and Pharisees and their systems are partly responsible for the woman's adultery. That the man is carefully avoided – he is not present, nor is he referred to by the accusers' words – is indicative of the male-dominant structures of society. Second, the accusers are invited to consider their own sin before judging the woman. *They cannot condemn her without admitting that they share her sinful nature.*

The words of Jesus bring about a complete reversal of things: the men who came feeling detached from the sinful woman have to enter into a relational understanding of sin, and they cannot neglect their own sin in order to understand the sin of the woman.

2 The antagonists realize their own sin

Let us explore this a little further. The words of Jesus obviously lead the accusers to a fresh realization. Their initial actions show clearly that they felt they had nothing do with this woman, and indeed, that they have nothing to do with sin at all. They see the evil in others, but not in themselves.

Jesus' words are not primarily an appeal to the law – either the law of Moses or that of the Roman state. In other circumstances, Jesus and elite groups do have arguments, but the focus here is not to win an argument; rather it is to save a woman who is condemned. Jesus appeals directly to the personal conscience of the accusers, although this appeal is accompanied by a warning to those who are with sin, but still try to judge others. Such a 'holier than thou' attitude is rebuked. We see the force with which Jesus' words strike the antagonists. They are convicted by conscience and no longer interested in the woman's sin as they must think about their own. The group takes the matter very personally; they realize how they have been behaving and that is the reason they begin to drift away. Verse 9 says that they left the place beginning with the elders or the older ones, and there may be some significance in the narrator's emphasis on this.

The scribes and Pharisees had come with the idea that they did not have any sin, or that their sin was so insignificant that they could condemn the woman. Now they have come to an understanding that they cannot talk about the sin of others without being aware of their own. They have moved from an unthought-through, stubborn position to a realization that they are sinful.

3 The antagonists retract from their determination to harm

We also see that the scribes and Pharisees pull back from their original purposes when they come into contact with the words of Jesus. They came to lynch the woman and trap Jesus, but they leave without doing either.

Significantly, there is a difference between opponents testing Jesus here and elsewhere. Usually they are trying to prove a point, or show that Jesus is wrong, or stop him from healing people. This is the only instance of Jesus being present when his opponents want to do something directly and immediately to a person, that is, where there is a victim.

There is no talk of a trial for the woman at all. It appears that the scribes and Pharisees are confident of taking the law into their own hands. As far as they are concerned, the woman has already been judged, and Jesus only has to pronounce her punishment. They are so determined that the woman should be condemned, that they persist with Jesus even when he does not say anything. They want to accomplish something without a doubt.

What eventually happens is that they have to retract. In a Jewish context, leaving one caught in adultery unpunished would not be possible because adultery brought a heavy penalty. Yet the scribes and Pharisees are reminded by Jesus that they cannot harm the woman, so they slip away without doing so.

The scribes and Pharisees might have left because their testing of

Jesus failed, but in fact they had the courage and self-awareness to realize their mistakes. They could have ignored the words of Jesus and killed the woman, but they did not do that. It is easy to accuse the scribes and Pharisees for trying to condemn the woman. We appreciate Jesus' way of handling them, but are we learning what we can from the changing attitudes they reveal? At least for a while, they received and responded to the words of Jesus; they related to the sinful woman, realizing their own sin and retracted from harming her. Taking seriously the words 'let anyone among you without sin be the first to cast their stone' is indeed crucial for the process of reconciliation and building relationships.

The story does not say that in the end the scribes and Pharisees reconciled with Jesus or with the woman, but the very fact that they did not harm her might be regarded as the beginning of reconciliation, and the story vividly conveys how realization and self-criticism can halt conflicts from escalating further.

A generous response to these antagonists for what they *try* to do to the woman and to Jesus may be difficult for us, because we find it easy to identify with Jesus and with the forgiven woman. In reality we may be worse than the antagonists, for we often condemn others and want them to be punished. How important not to lose the element of self-criticism – we have something to learn from the antagonists, indeed!

Questions for reflection

1 Are we part of the 'no one' (verse 11) referred to by the woman Jesus loved and forgave?
2 Do we take the words of Jesus seriously when tempted to pass judgment on others?
3 We may think that we are better than the people who sin in the Bible. Why and how should we overcome such attitudes?

21 Am I God? A study in contrast

Key texts:

- **Genesis 30.1–2**
- **2 Kings 5.5–8**
- **Genesis 50.15–21**

Key characters studied:

- Jacob
- Jehoram, the King of Israel
- Joseph

'Am I God?' is an interesting expression to reflect upon in thinking about reconciliation. In the Old Testament, this question is always asked in the context of tension and broken relationships or relationships that are about to be broken. The phrase is expanded variously such as, 'Am I in the place God?', 'Can I act for God?', 'Can I put myself in God's place?' and so on.

Before we consider this further, let us be clear that an attitude of 'I am God' or 'I am in the place of God' is detrimental to human relationships and will not help in the process of reconciliation. There are a number of biblical personalities who exalted themselves to the position of God and ruined their lives and those of people around them. In the political history of the world, one often comes across such approaches and the inevitable destruction that follows.

In contrast, the question 'Am I God?' at first seems quite polite and humble. We might think it would be helpful for building relationships between human beings. However, the Bible reveals that it has been used in a number of different ways.

This expression of affirmative negation is considered an important figure of speech in the Bible. Questions such as 'is anything too difficult for God?' and 'will God stay silent for ever?', where the expected answer is 'no', are examples. As we can see, the question is put in the affirmative, but the answer to be offered will certainly be in the negative.

Am I God? Anger and frustration in Jacob

Jacob asks this question to his wife Rachel to express his frustration in Genesis 30.2, which reads: *Jacob became very angry with Rachel and said, 'Am I in the place of God, who has withheld from you the fruit of the womb?'*

The story is familiar: Jacob loves Rachel and wants to marry her, but is cheated by her father Laban into first marrying her sister Leah. In due course, Rachel becomes Jacob's second wife. God sees that Leah is despised and unloved and blesses her with children, but then Rachel complains to Jacob: give me children, or I shall die. Jacob responds with 'Am I God?', which expresses his frustration, irritation, anger and, possibly, a bit of arrogance.

In fact, Jacob is completely right when he says that God has withheld the fruit of Rachel's womb because the Old Testament understanding is that children are a blessing from God. Jacob is clearly expressing that he cannot act for God, but the frustration and anger present in his reply to Rachel rather undermines his affirmation of God's power. Let us also consider that Rachel could have prayed to God as Hannah would do later (see 1 Samuel 1), instead of envying Leah and complaining bitterly. Jacob could also have prayed for his wife, as his father Isaac did for his wife Rebecca, when she too was facing childlessness (Genesis 25.21). It is a pity that Jacob did not think of taking the matter to God, or of answering Rachel kindly – after all, being childless was shameful and humiliating for her. Jacob seems to fail to understand his wife's distress. Shouting at her 'Am I God?' may actually indicate a kind of arrogance that 'if I were God, I would see to things'. In other words, even though God's power is affirmed in Jacob's expression of 'Am I God?', there is a hint of looking for an immediate solution, rather than waiting for God to act.

Am I God? Fear in the king of Israel

In a second context, we see this phrase used to express fear. We read in 2 Kings 5.7:

> When the king of Israel read the letter, he tore his clothes and said, 'Am I God, to give death or life, that this man sends word to me to cure a man of his leprosy? Just look and see how he is trying to pick a quarrel with me.'

These are the words of the king of Israel, believed to be Jehoram. Naaman, the commander of the Syrian army who is affected by leprosy, learns from his wife's slave girl (whose courage we read of in study 16) about the prophet Elisha in Israel who can heal him. Namaan obtains a letter from his king and comes to the king of Israel. (It was quite common in those times for kings to send letters to one another for healing purposes.) However, the latter, in suspicion and fear, tears his clothes and speaks the words we read above.

Jehoram was right in saying that he cannot kill or give life, for only God can do that. We read in Deuteronomy 32.39 that 'to kill and to make alive' always belonged to God. At the outset it appears that Jehoram, like Jacob, is affirming God. However, the king of Israel's doubts about God are plain to see. Although a slave girl (in exile in Syria) can trust in God's prophets, the king fails to believe that they are already there in Israel. Like Jacob, Jehoram does not appeal to God to act, or bother to wait for God to do so, but hastily shreds his clothes. The tearing of royal robes is a sign of national mourning, and Jehoram speeds to this stage. He does not look back at the saving works of God in Israel; he does not want to affirm that God is already at work in Israel. In his impulsive behaviour, the king does not even think to send Naaman to Elisha for healing. It is clear that Jehoram may have believed in the power of God to kill and make alive, but he fails to acknowledge God's continuing work in Israel.

We have now seen two instances of people referring to the power and the omnipotence of God, who nevertheless fail to affirm or understand the way in which God acts or respond to the needs of their fellow human beings. One utters 'Am I God?' to expresses frustration and the other to express fear.

Now let us turn to an occasion – the reconciliation of Joseph and his brothers – where this expression is used very positively and in a way that affirms relationship.

Am I God? Reconciliation in Joseph

We read in Genesis 50.19–20: 'But Joseph said to them, "Do not be afraid! Am I in the place of God? Even though you intended to do harm to me, God intended it for good, in order to preserve a numerous people, as he is doing today." '

We know Joseph's story. When we come to Genesis 50, we see that Joseph has already forgiven his brothers for selling him into slavery – he did so when he revealed himself to them (45.1). However, his brothers are still feeling guilty, and when Jacob dies they fear that

Joseph may turn against them. He may have been silent so far so as not to distress his father, his brothers think. Now that Jacob is dead he may take revenge, but when his brothers approach Joseph for forgiveness, Joseph tells them 'do not be afraid, am I God?'

In contrast to the earlier narratives, the phrase 'am I God' is uttered here in friendship, fellowship and forgiveness. More importantly, Joseph's affirmation of God and God's power is expressed in a very positive way. He weeps (Genesis 50.17) because his brothers thought they would need mediators and offers them comforting and encouraging words, 'do not be afraid'. He acknowledges how God has been at work through him and through his brothers. Although they behaved in an evil manner towards him, God has turned their actions to good. Not only Joseph's relationship with God, but also that of his brothers, have been used in God's saving act. Joseph, who all his life has been waiting for God to act, believes that *God is already in action*.

In Jacob's and Jehoram's utterances, the expression 'am I God' suggests the possibility that 'if I were in God's place, I could have done this, or I could do this'. Yet there is no such suggestion with Joseph. For him, it is not the question of 'if I were in God's place', but of what has to be done towards God. His words to his brothers might be rephrased like this: 'I am not God, so you do not need to bow down before me, and you do not need to be afraid of me. Let me not take the praise and glory that is due to God alone.'

'Am I God?' has revealed much about how each person we looked at waited or did not wait for God to act. Jacob does not want to talk to Rachel about holding on for God's time to come, and to remember how his father and grandfather handled a similar situation. Jehoram does not want to look for the prophet of God who can heal Naaman. However, Joseph patiently affirms how God in God's own time has reversed the evil done to him to good, for the sake of many.

Jacob and Jehoram do not relate to their own selves well, as the anger and fear within them are wrongly directed. They do not relate well with their fellow-human beings either, and their affirmation of God is marked by disbelief and arrogance. However, Joseph, believing in God, humbly reaffirms the reconciliation that has taken place between him and his brothers to strengthen the relationships between them.

Questions for reflection

1   In our personal relationships, do we ever come close to asking the question 'am I God'? In what circumstances might we do so? Does asking this help us to humble ourselves and build relationships with our fellow human beings, or are we conveying frustration, anger or fear?

2   Think about similar instances of the expression of humility towards others in the Bible. For instance, Peter says to Cornelius in Acts 10.26: 'Stand up; I am only a mortal'.

3   Has this study been an encouragement to you in your ministry of reconciliation and, if so, how?

22 Who is my neighbour?

Key text: Luke 10.25–37
The lawyer's question and Jesus' parable of the Good Samaritan

The Good Samaritan story is one of the most interesting parables Jesus told. It emphasizes the importance of extending love and care to others, and it reveals that our status in our community need not be a hindrance to doing so. The direct single message we receive is that we should strive to become a Good Samaritan, guided by the perfect Good Samaritan, our Lord Jesus Christ, who has given everything for us.

We should notice in this passage that there are some seemingly unconnected questions and responses. The question asked by the lawyer and the answers provided by Jesus are not directly related. The lawyer asks, who is his neighbour, but Jesus talks about a wounded man whose identity is not revealed, a Samaritan who comes to the man's assistance and other individuals who do not, before finally asking some counter-questions.

Although the lawyer's question to Jesus, 'who is my neighbour?', seems linked to the idea of relationship, it is framed in such a way that the lawyer keeps himself at the centre and relegates others to a lesser position. He actually asks the question to justify himself. Self-justification is not helpful in relating to one's neighbours and Jesus challenges this attitude.

Jesus tells the story of the Good Samaritan to show that the question the lawyer asked is wrongly conceived. It misleads in its suggestion of how relationships may be constructed. Instead of offering a direct answer, Jesus invites the lawyer to deny himself, showing that it is not by asking 'who is my neighbour?', but by *becoming* a neighbour for others that we build relationships and bring about reconciliation.

1 Who is my *neighbour*?

'And who is my neighbour?' is the actual question the lawyer asks (verse 29), suggesting a connection to what has happened previously in the text. We see in verse 25 that the lawyer wants to test Jesus and enquires 'what must I do to inherit eternal life'. Jesus counters with 'What is written in the law? What do you read there?' and the lawyer provides the answer: 'You shall love the Lord your God with all your

93

heart, and with all your soul, and with all your strength, and with all your mind, and your neighbour as yourself.' Jesus then commands the lawyer to do what is in the law. We may think the episode is over, but the lawyer is not inclined to stop there. He is seeking validation – or praise? – and so he throws another question: 'Who is my neighbour?' It seems the lawyer is saying, okay Jesus, I will love my neighbours as myself, but tell me who my neighbour is so that I can extend my love. I am a Jew and a lawyer and thus in a position to help others. The only thing you need tell me is who my neighbour is.

The lawyer might actually have asked the question to irritate Jesus as well as to test him. We read in several places in the Old Testament that the Israelite understanding of neighbours was very limited. Mostly, the neighbours of Israelites were fellow Israelites (see Leviticus 19.18), with other people generally termed strangers or gentiles. Quite apart from this narrow perception of one's neighbour, the lawyer's question is egotistical and arrogant. I am there to help, he tells Jesus, but show me whom I should help.

Jesus' response is to tell a story involving a Samaritan. Samaritans were generally despised by Jews at that time, but Jesus shows how this man, regarded as being of lower status, could offer help to a wounded man. He is saying that it is not only Jews who can extend help, but that Samaritans can too. In this way, he challenges the self-proclaimed supremacy of the lawyer.

Jesus also overturns the lawyer's understanding of a neighbour – as one who is in need of help, an object of benevolent action. He shows that a neighbour is actually someone in relationship to another person, and (as we saw above) that the neighbour may actually be the one who helps a person in need.

2   Who is *my* neighbour?

The lawyer's question 'who is *my* neighbour' reveals that the lawyer wants to know his neighbour from the perspective of his superior status so that he can do the necessary loving.

Yet Jesus does not talk about the lawyer's neighbour in his response. In fact, Jesus never talks about a neighbour in terms of one to whom help should be extended. If he had, the question he asked at the end of the parable would more likely have been, who was a neighbour to the Samaritan, who was able to help? – to which the answer would be the wounded man. This would have justified the lawyer's question, but

Jesus actually asks, 'who was the neighbour to the wounded man?' and thus illustrates that the lawyer's question fails to promote proper understanding of one's neighbour. A neighbour should be understood from the perspective of a person who is in a desperate condition and needs help. Jesus invites the lawyer to see that the wounded man regarded the Samaritan as a neighbour. Getting his help was a matter of life and death.

The lawyer has difficulty understanding others because he cannot rid himself of the notion that he is a superior being. He wants *to know others through himself*, keeping himself at the centre, but Jesus teaches him *to understand himself through others*. The lawyer's question is centred on himself, while Jesus' answer is centred on the wounded man and the Samaritan who helped him. For the lawyer, this might have seemed very odd, but Jesus is more concerned to correct his mindset than to answer or justify his question.

In our own lives, we mostly try to understand others through ourselves. We are always proud of what we have achieved, and in relationships we (perhaps subconsciously) stress the importance of our time, our generosity, our love . . . It is all about us. As Jesus taught the lawyer, the better, though very challenging way, is to try to understand ourselves through others.

3 *Who* is my neighbour?

In his question '*who* is my neighbour', the lawyer is interested in getting some hard information. We sense he wants a fixed and certain answer. The way in which he puts the question also suggests that he expects there to be neighbours and non-neighbours.

Jesus does not provide any information with regard to *who* a neighbour is, though. His final answer comes not in noun, but in verb form and it invites the lawyer to take action: to go and do as the Samaritan did. In other words, to know who your neighbour is you *become* a neighbour to others. The lawyer wants to know who his neighbour is. Jesus shows him *what* he should do to become a neighbour. The lawyer wants to know who a neighbour is so that he can show love, but Jesus shows that by loving you become a neighbour to others.

The Greek term used in verse 36 is *gegonenai* (to have become). Jesus shifts the focus of the question to ask: *who had become* a neighbour to the wounded man? So not, 'who is my neighbour?'

but 'to whom have I to become a neighbour?' As we have seen, the lawyer's question requests definition, while Jesus' response focuses on action.

We look for fixed answers to our problems, we want things to be clear, but binary thinking can blind us to the truth of the matter, that we are invited *to be and to become*. We do not really need to ask who our neighbour is; we do not need to be told whom to love and care for. We know that by becoming a neighbour to others, neighbourliness will grow. The lawyer asked who is my neighbour? Jesus made him realize the real question is: how I should *become* a neighbour to others?

In the context of the Christian ministry of reconciliation, the Good Samaritan parable teaches us that we should not assume we know who our neighbours will turn out to be. When we do that, we tend to find neighbours only in communities that are identical to ours. While it is fair to say that relationships based on commonality may help us practically, as disciples of Christ we are invited to move beyond the familiar and comforting to become neighbours to others. As one theologian aptly puts it, 'Neighbourhood does not create love, but love creates a neighbourhood.' The Good Samaritan parable tells us that we shall come to know our neighbours in the course of our life experiences, not forgetting that to get good neighbours we have to be good neighbours. Let us thus not attempt to define our neighbours, but in all humility and openness, let us become neighbours to one another.

Questions for reflection

1 In relating to others, do you feel you often keep yourself at the centre? If so, why might this be?
2 Has this study made you aware of a tendency to categorize people into neighbours and non-neighbours?
3 Why is looking for fixed answers to whom we should befriend problematic?

23 'She is more in the right than I!'

Key text: Genesis 38
Judah and Tamar

Imagine that you are in a powerful position when a conflict occurs between you and someone else, and it transpires that you are responsible for the crisis. What would you do? Most of us would probably rush to deny our role in the conflict – being more powerful than the other person, of course, giving us an advantage. Phrases such as 'It was your mistake!', 'You only escalated the problem' and 'I've done nothing wrong' are common in this kind of context. However, denying one's role tends to bring any effort at reconciliation to a dead end. It is rare, when a relationship has broken down, to hear statements like, 'What I did was wrong' or 'It was at least as much my fault as yours', and it is an exception to find such words even in the Bible. However, something of this sort is uttered by Judah, in whose tribe Jesus was born.

Genesis 38 tells the story of Tamar being cheated by Judah. Judah appears in this story after he successfully persuades his brothers not to kill Joseph, but to sell him to the Ishmaelites who are on their way to Egypt. At this point, Judah is supposed to be giving his third son Selah to Tamar in marriage. His first son Er married Tamar, but the Lord was displeased with him, so he died. Then Onan, according to the custom of the time, in what was known as levirate marriage law, is asked to raise up offspring for his dead brother through Tamar. Yet Onan is not interested in helping Tamar bear children as any born would not be his. This displeases God, and Onan also dies, leaving Tamar again without a husband.

Now, fearing that his third son Selah might also die, Judah sends Tamar to her father's house to remain as a widow until Selah grows up (verse 11). When Tamar sees that Selah is an adult (and she still has not been given to him in marriage), she decides to 'deceive' her father-in-law. She acts as a prostitute to Judah, lies with him without Judah realizing she is his daughter-in-law, and becomes pregnant. She shrewdly makes sure to collect Judah's signet, cord and staff from him. When Tamar's pregnancy becomes known, Judah is angry that she has behaved as a prostitute and is ready to kill her, but his daughter-in-law has evidence that he is the father of the unborn child. When

Judah sees his personal possessions, he realizes and acknowledges his mistakes, saying 'she is more in the right than I'. This is definitely one of the most powerful statements that can ever be made in a conflict situation.

It appears in the story that Tamar deceives Judah, but it is actually Judah who deceives her by not giving her his third son Selah, as it was his duty to do. Tamar wants her birth right, but Judah has made her stay at her father's house as a widow, and does not have any intention of improving her circumstances. Some Christians may feel uncomfortable about Tamar's subsequent actions, although Judah's words vindicate her in the end. Our focus should perhaps be more on Judah's attitudes than on Tamar's character, although she is often celebrated (correctly!) as a heroine who saved the line of Judah – which produced king David and later the Messiah.

First, we should understand that Judah was genuinely afraid that he would lose his youngest, and now only, son. He may have felt that Tamar was unlucky, having had two husbands who had predeceased her. Judah, however, bears some responsibility for his sons' fate. If he had taught them to live in godly ways, they would not have displeased God and died.

Second, when Tamar produces her evidence, Judah, without any fuss or explanation, simply acknowledges that the signet, cord and staff are his. He does not analyse how Tamar ended up with his stuff. He is quick to realize that he is responsible for Tamar's condition although he has just been in a hurry to judge and punish her. He is not prevented by fear of what others might think from publicly admitting his mistake.

Of course, it could be that Judah did this because he was caught fair and square and had no other option. I don't think this is the case. It would take courage to admit to what he did and to acknowledge his mistakes. This is someone who has given the judgement that 'she should be killed', but the judge quickly realizes not only that he has given a wrong judgement, but also that he bears ultimate responsibility for this crisis.

Third, Judah not only admits that the things Tamar presents are his and that he is responsible for her pregnancy; he expresses an exemplary, self-critical attitude. He *fully* takes responsibility and concedes that what he did has led to this situation. He shows a sense of accountability. He does not look for reasons for the crisis outside himself. We may not find it difficult to be critical of ourselves when we pray to God or confess our sins; however, it is not at all easy to be self-critical to a fellow human being. It is humiliating. Judah, though, is openly critical of himself in public.

The words 'she is more in the right than I' (verse 26) have some significance here. They are comparative, but Judah is not seeking to show who is more righteous, relatively speaking. Rather, the implied meaning is that Tamar is *not at all* the one responsible for this crisis. Judah conveys the message that he – and he alone – is to blame. He does not make excuses, and his candid admittance of error importantly solves a crisis once and for all.

Fourth, Judah's self-critical attitude leads to better treatment for the victim. Tamar is in a life or death situation, but Judah defuses the tension. Tamar has not received the husband she should have been given, and Judah acknowledges this. When caught, he does not speak of Tamar in a negative light. He does not say that she was after sex. He does not say that she was an adulteress, playing the whore to everyone, including Judah. It is worth noting that he is not showing pity to Tamar because of her condition, rather his focus is squarely on what he did. In being critical of himself, Judah behaves rightly and justly towards the other, which is very important in the context of reconciliation.

Tamar confronts and dares Judah. She indirectly tells him that what she did was right. Judah has been concerned about her crime and how she should be punished; Tamar is interested only in who is responsible for her pregnancy. Her 'take note, please' (verse 25) is a direct challenge to him, but Judah does not attempt to criminalize or demean her to protect himself. It might have been easy for him to do that given the patriarchal context. He could have said you lied, you cheated, you played the whore, and so on, but Judah is self-critical enough to treat Tamar better than himself.

Living in a time when we tend to rush to accuse someone, even when we do not know if they are guilty, what Judah does is great. He takes the entire blame himself. For me, Judah very openly lives up to how Paul would later urge the Philippines to act: 'Do nothing from selfish ambition or conceit, but in humility regard others as better than yourselves' (Philippians 2.3). Judah is an example of someone who affirms the righteousness of the other in a conflict, which leads to reconciliation.

Questions for reflection

1 Why is self-criticism essential in solving conflicts? How often are we willing to treat others better than ourselves?

2 When we are in the wrong, are we ready to acknowledge this directly to the victim in public, rather than admitting it secretly (perhaps only to God)?

3 How do we respond when someone challenges our mistakes? If we rush to accuse them in return, how might we act differently?

24 The king who humbled himself

Key text: 2 Chronicles 33
Manasseh's reconciliation with God

As Christians, we probably all have atheist friends with whom we argue about the existence of God. Whether we can ever 'prove' there is a God – and our friends can ever prove there is no God – is a different matter. As Christians, how do we affirm God? What do we mean when we say we believe in God? How do we demonstrate or live out our belief in God? Do we believe just because *we say* we believe? Are spoken words and written and signed declarations sufficient? I doubt we think so. These may be helpful for institutional purposes in our churches and Christian organizations, but believing in God basically involves a personal relationship – one in which what we *do* with our 'self' is the most important thing.

Believing in God is affirmation through action – mere words are not sufficient to express our belief. As the Bible shows us from beginning to end, one of the primary ways to believe in God and to connect with God is by knowing our place as human beings in relation to God. This involves understanding that we are not, and cannot be, on our own in life (although we may certainly develop self-confidence, which we surely need). Believing in God involves being aware of our shortcomings and limitations as human beings, and realizing that we are dependent on the Other who is above, beneath, within and surrounding us (as well as being dependent on those with whom we share the world). In other words, an attitude of humility is vital to believing in and affirming God.

This is evident when we look at God's dealings with God's people throughout history, as recorded in the Bible. In Micah 6.8, humility stands out as one of the three primary attitudes God expects from human beings. One of the main reasons that relationships break down is because of human beings' never-ending desire to exalt themselves over everything. When we exalt ourselves over God and become arrogant, the result is conflict between us and God, and among ourselves.

This study is on Manasseh, a unique king in the history of Judah, who does everything to displease God and earn God's anger, but who is restored to relationship with God when he is offered – and takes –

an opportunity to humble himself. (There are, of course, two versions of his story, and the one in the Book of Kings (2 Kings 21) does not have the glorious ending of the story in Chronicles.)

1 Humility: the essential factor between God and the kings

It is generally understood that kings (or any kind of leader) should be magnanimous. Greatness, confidence and the mastering of various skills may be seen as a vital part of magnanimity – all are needed to rule people well. However, the past and present show us that many kings and leaders have often been proud, arrogant, disconnected from others and contemptuous of those they rule. Such leaders have caused the destruction of millions of people. However, the presence of a certain amount of pride and arrogance in leaders may be justified; many believe these are required to build self-esteem. We live at a time when some governments spend a great amount of money to boost the psychological health of political leaders, so although feelings of lowliness, weakness and ordinariness naturally still exist in those elevated to such roles, the necessary strength to lead may be brought to the fore.

In the Bible, God's dealings with people – and with kings – are always based on their ability to humble themselves before God. However, this has proved very challenging for humanity in general and even more so for kings and leaders. You can imagine that being a king and being humble is not easy. Yet when we read God's conversations with kings in the Old Testament, they are full of demands for humility. Pride, arrogance and exalting themselves before God were serious problems – no more so than for the kings in Judah and Israel in the first half of the first millennium BC, who were often in conflict with God.

2 Humility and the kings: Manasseh's humility in comparison

When it comes to an attitude of humility, we generally have two types of king in the Old Testament – those who never humbled themselves before God, and those who were humble in the beginning, but then ran into difficulties and began exalting themselves. Perhaps Manasseh is the only king who stands out as different: he was horrible for a long time, but at the end of his life is filled with humility, which makes possible his reconciliation with God.

Even some of the best kings were a problem. David, in spite of being close to God's heart, did many things which displeased God. He lusted after Bathsheba and murdered her husband Uriah (2 Samuel 11) and he took a census, which was obviously a step to estimate his strength. Instead of depending on God's guidance and strength, he displayed pride and arrogance. Solomon, the wisest king Israel ever had, began to reject God and God's words towards the end, which ultimately led to the division of the kingdom (1 Kings 11). Another good king, Hezekiah, depended on God and sought God's help when the Assyrian king came against him in war (2 Kings 18–19). He prayed to God for his life when the prophet Isaiah told him that he would die and was granted some more years (2 Kings 20.1–11). Yet when the envoys from the king of Babylon came to visit him, Hezekiah earned the wrath of God by showing them his might and strength (i.e. his weapons and wealth) (2 Kings 20.12–19). Josiah, who was known for his reforms for Yahweh in Judah (2 Kings 22–23; 2 Chronicles 34–35) rejected God's words at the end of his life, became unnecessarily involved in a war with the king of Egypt and was killed (2 Chronicles 35.20–24).

Manasseh was one of the wickedest kings of Judah, however. He did everything to provoke God's anger and drive people away from God (2 Kings 33.1–10). Could reconciliation even be possible for such a depraved king? For God, yes – if there is humility! Manasseh's story reveals that for God, no one is beyond hope. He was wicked, but he was willing to humble himself when he was in trouble. Perhaps the only other wicked king who does occasionally humble himself is Ahab, the king of Israel (1 Kings 21.27), but Manasseh's case is fairly unique.

3 Manasseh's humility, reconciliation and restoration

Manasseh also clearly demonstrates belated reconciliation. When Manasseh is at his worst, he is tied and taken to Babylon. This is very humiliating for a king, and it gives Manasseh the chance to turn to and reconcile with God. He grabs the opportunity, and we read that he entreats the Lord *his* God (2 Chronicles 33.12). Manasseh's story shows that humility before God makes reconciliation with God possible. His humility has some interesting consequences.

First, God brings him back to Jerusalem as king and his kingdom is restored. (The only other king to be restored to his kingdom was

David, but that was when he was fleeing Absalom. After Absalom is killed David eventually comes back.) Manasseh is a great example of humility in a king making reconciliation with God, and restoration by God, possible. Importantly, Manasseh is given the longest number of years, 55, to rule his country – more than any other king in Judah or Israel.

Second, Manasseh's humility marks him out as an example to the kings who come after him. His humility is a talking point even many years after his death. 2 Chronicles 33.23 speaks about Amon, Manasseh's son, saying he did not humble himself, unlike his father Manasseh. When compared to all other kings, Manasseh stands out as an example of what matters most to God: how a king finishes his life rather how he began it.

Questions for reflection

1 Why is humility regarded as the most important virtue in God-human relations?
2 How do we exercise humility, especially when we are in positions of leadership?
3 What are the obstacles to exercising humility before God and others in our lives?

25 Be a servant: a way to build relationships

Key text: Matthew 20.20–28
Jesus' response to the conflicts among his disciples

When we see pictures or videos of seemingly delicate animals attacking powerful ones, they surprise us. We have notions of strong animals and weak animals, with the lion often being regarded as the king of the jungle. However, the arrival of advanced technology allows us to observe animal behaviour very closely and reveals how one species may relate to another. Social media posts often show us videos of animals we would normally regard as prey for 'strong' ones actually being the aggressors (for instance, buffalo attacking and even killing a lion). When I read the reactions and comments of viewers, I find they sometimes express (understandable) disbelief, but I have also noticed an uneasiness about weak animals overpowering strong ones. People wonder whether such a thing *should* happen: there is a feeling that it is unacceptable due to the notion that the weak should submit to the powerful, who may behave with pride and arrogance (characteristics of power). We may think this also applies to human life and relations, but it is a fact that aspiring to power in order to dominate others leads to conflict (unlike in the animal world, where the fight is either for prey or to escape becoming prey). Jesus taught and showed that becoming great and 'powerful' does not involve exercising dominance and pride over others. Rather, seeking power in the context of human community encompasses living in good relationship with one another and continuing to build such relationships.

In spite of listening to and witnessing Jesus' efforts to reconcile human beings with God and with one another, his disciples were not exempt from conflict. They came from various walks of life and so had different cultural, social and economic backgrounds. We quite often see them caught up in quarrels, and occasionally they are furious with one another. The future leaders of the ministry of reconciliation themselves in need of reconciliation! Generally, their conflicts relate to the anticipation of power – for themselves or over others. However, Jesus is clear that this model will not work. He has to reconcile them sometimes and demonstrates that only through servanthood will they be able to relate with one another.

105

For example, on one occasion Zebedee's wife comes to ask if her sons, James and John, could sit on the right and left hand of Jesus in his kingdom. The other disciples are enraged. Attempting to reconcile them, Jesus points out how the Gentile rulers govern their people – in a way that dominates and undermines others and causes conflict – and says that it should not be so among the disciples. Such a model cannot support Christian discipleship or Christian community.

Let us return to Jesus' alternative – the model of servanthood. This involves not simply being of service, but also being open to suffering in order to serve others. It means being meek when we would like to be assertive and embracing lowliness when we would prefer to feel powerful. Jesus never hesitated to enter into lowliness in his life and death. The questions he asked, 'Why do you call me good? No one is good but God alone' (Mark 10.18; Luke 18.19) and his washing of his disciples' feet are examples of this. Jesus shows that servanthood can help to build relationships in a community. Instead of lording it over others, servanthood helps us relate to and reconcile with one another and to avoid conflict (which is closely connected to seeking power).

Sometimes we come across the argument that conflict can be beneficial to society and enable the growth of community. There may be truth in this. The conflict between Paul and Barnabas (Acts 15.36–39) is often cited as facilitating the spread of the early church. However, there is a difference between a conflcit that leads to bitterness, hate and violence and a conflict in the context of disagreement (where respect is not lost and the other is not diminished). The first is often caused by the rejection of the other and the anticipation of power and domination, and Jesus is clearly against anything that undermines or derides our brothers and sisters. Disagreement, on the other hand, need not involve disrespect: we can disagree with someone but still esteem them. It is worth mentioning here that Jesus does not endorse avoiding conflict if this involves keeping silent when injustice is being carried out against the disadvantaged around us.

Of course, one may wonder how practising servanthood will help in building relationships. We may fear being neglected, undermined or ignored, but our everyday experience is that power and egotism are not good alternatives. (The irony of living in a world of 'peace-keeping-forces' will not be lost on us. Although the vulnerable in conflict zones may be glad to have troops to offer them relief, we seem to see more of the force and less of the peace.) So what did Jesus teach his disciples?

He wanted them to understand that you cannot think of power without considering how it might contribute to community. Or to put this slightly differently, how do we think of power in the context of Christian servanthood? Duane Elmer says:

> Power is meant to be shared with the goal of empowering others. Hoarded power weakens others and exalts oneself. Power, when grounded in biblical values, serves others by liberating them. It acknowledges that people bear the image of God and treats them in a way that will nurture the development of that image. In so doing, we honor their Creator.
>
> (*Cross-Cultural Servanthood: Serving the World in Christlike Humility*)

Servanthood is built on other-centredness and not on self-centredness. St Augustine said that God's own humility, revealed in an act of divine grace, is the only reference point for Christian servanthood. Imitating this 'lowly God' is the foundation of Christian existence.

Jesus challenges us, as he did his disciples, to model servanthood in order to help build and re-build communities and to bring reconciliation to broken relationships.

Questions for reflection

1 In what *practical* ways can we model servanthood to build relationships in communities and heal wounds in broken relationships?
2 What helps you distinguish between a conflict and a disagreement?
3 Think further on why a Christian understanding of power must be concerned with the well-being of everyone in a community.

26 The problem with those who claim they see

Key text: John 9
Jesus, the blind man and the Pharisees

While Jesus came to reconcile humanity with God and human beings with one another, one group repeatedly found itself unable to accept Jesus and his message: the religious leaders around him. John 9 gives us an insight into why this was so. We learn from the miracle story of the healing of the blind man that, among other things, the religious leaders had a completely mistaken understanding of sin, and this affected the way in which they related to God, to Jesus and to their fellow human beings.

The healing of the blind man happens to take place on a Sabbath day. When those around him come to know that he has been healed by Jesus, they take him to the Pharisees, who interrogate him. When the man testifies that Jesus has healed him, they turn him away, but Jesus embraces him saying, 'I came into this world for judgment so that those who do not see may see, and those who do see may become blind' (verse 39). Hearing this, the Pharisees ask Jesus if they are blind and Jesus tells them, 'If you were blind, you would not have sin. But now that you say, "We see," your sin remains' (verse 41).

This story offers a number of insights into the way in which sin affects our attitudes to others and our relationships with them. In fact, the disciples, the Pharisees, the healed man and Jesus each express their views on sin differently. Jesus corrects the disciples and challenges the Pharisees, for the latter are stubbornly unwilling to learn from his teaching and works.

Interestingly, the story begins with the disciples asking Jesus whose sin has caused the blindness of the man. Is it his own sin or that of his parents? In verse 3, Jesus clearly states that sin cannot be linked to physical disability. This is a very powerful response, indicating that sin is not hereditary in nature, passing on from one generation to another. Jesus avoids further discussion of sin in relation to the blind man and says that he was born for God's name to be glorified. Thus, the chapter begins with an understanding that sin is not connected with being physically blind, but ends with Jesus telling the Pharisees that their claiming to see – even as they undermine others and live in broken relationships with God and with the rest of society – is in fact sin.

1 Their sin remains because they claim they see

The Pharisees think they see and, in their world, that only they can see and others cannot. As long as they claim they see, they remain blind and cannot be reconciled with others. Their claiming to see relates to their attitude of arrogance, and a lack of humility among the Pharisees is something that Jesus challenges quite often. The prayer of the Pharisee in Luke 18.9–14 is a case in point. The Pharisees have always believed that what they do is correct and how they interpret the law is the final word on the matter. They think they are always right, they are right in everything, and only they are right. Yet while they look for sin everywhere else (such as in physical disability or in the violation of the Law of Moses), Jesus says that they need to look for sin within themselves. It is because of their arrogant attitude that their sin remains.

We often act as the Pharisees do. We claim we see, but we remain blind and sinful because of our pride and lack of humility. The worst sin is to claim one is sinless. John in one of his letters says clearly: 'If we say that we have not sinned, we make him [God] a liar, and his word is not in us.' (1 John 1.10).

2 They are eager to see what they do not need to see

The Pharisees' way of seeing is not right. They see in others what they don't need to see and spend a lot of time talking about the sin of others. They clearly use one scale for themselves and one for everyone else. What they should actually see is their own sin. They also try to find fault with Jesus for healing on the Sabbath.

The healed man's answer in verse 27 is interesting. His 'I do not know if he is a sinner' reveals that he is not concerned about judging whether others are sinful or not; he is simply revelling in the fact that he *was* blind and now he can see. The Pharisees return to their preoccupation; they spend a lot of time discussing whether Jesus was a sinner, and quickly dismiss the healed man as 'fully born in sin'. While they are doing this, they think they see and that they are the only ones to see, but they are actually blind.

In our own lives and ministry, we are often more concerned about others' sin and their repentance than ours, and I think this is one of the serious problems with contemporary Christianity. In Christian mission, I often see the need for repentance for sins being regarded as a distinguishing point between Christians and non-Christians. We do not seem too concerned about our own role in keeping slavery, servitude, racism and other forms of discrimination alive for our own benefit. We do not worry that our economic and business plans affect huge numbers of people. We do not cry out against supporting arms sales which kill millions. Yet we keep repentance stored for 'those who do not know Jesus Christ yet'. This attitude – that repentance is something lacking in others – has dominated global mission and has actually affected Christianity. In personal terms, we often rush to search for the location of sin *outside* us, even though we call ourselves sinners. Our own acts of repentance are meaningless if we allow injustices around us to continue because they happen to benefit us.

3 They were unwilling to see what they should see

The Pharisees claim they see, but they don't actually want to see the things they should see. They are unwilling to see what Jesus does; they only see as they want.

They are unwilling to accept the man. They didn't accept him as a blind man, and now they cannot accept the fact that he is a healed man. There should be great rejoicing because a miracle has taken place and a blind man now sees, but instead the Pharisees persist in trying to get the man to betray Jesus, and when that fails, they drive him away.

The Pharisees cannot reconcile with Jesus and the healed man, who now sees, because they themselves are blind. The sin here is not his blindness (physical), but their blindness (arrogance).

For ourselves, I believe our understanding of sin – in terms of who is right and who is wrong, who is sinful and who is holy – may be what drives our relationships with one another more than anything else. Among Christians, how we understand sin affects and divides people more than any other doctrine. Jesus, through his conversations with the Pharisees, helps us to perceive that it is because we claim we see (when we do not) and because we see the sin in others (but ignore our own) that we remain sinners. This considerably affects our relationship with God and with our fellow human beings, and is a barrier to reconciliation.

Questions for reflection

1 Reflect on a situation when you claimed you could see, but in retrospect realize you were actually blind.

2 How can we avoid seeing what we do not need to? How can we grow in genuine repentance for our sins?

3 When asked to respond to the comment that Jesus is a sinner, the blind man says, 'I do not know whether he is a sinner. One thing I do know, that though I was blind, now I see.' In what ways we can grow in seeing what we need to see?

6

Radical openness to the other

Reconciliation is a joyful experience and when we reach this stage we feel considerable pleasure. Nevertheless, reconciliation can be a slow and painful process, particularly if those involved do not aspire equally to having their differences resolved. Everyone has memories of wounds, hurts and suffering, and often we feel those who have wronged us should be punished. If the reconciliation process is to begin, however, someone has to take the initiative; someone has to step forward to get things moving. We saw in Chapter 4 that there are mediators who are willing to take the risk of reconciling hostile people and groups. However, such people are rare. (We are probably aware that our own involvement in reconciling others has been fairly limited.) To begin the process, someone has to break through boundaries to enter into the territory of another – and this other needs to be happy to welcome and embrace the first person, who may be quite reluctant to take steps into the other's space.

As we know, reconciliation is not only about mending broken relationships, but about building new ones. The latter involves being open to those who would normally have nothing to do with us, those whom we think of as completely different. This second kind of reconciliation is even more difficult than the first. We might perceive that an other is important, yet feel unable to bond with them.

Each religious tradition emerges as a reaction to what is going on in the world, and each tries to influence and change that condition through a focus on God or the Supreme Being or the Absolute, or whatever name is used. Christianity attempts to change how people relate to God and to their fellow human beings. If the whole essence of Christianity were to be summarized in two words, they would be 'radical openness'. The Trinity displays radical openness between the Father, the Son and the Holy Spirit and towards the entire creation. God's openness to the other, fully expressed to the world though God's revelation in Christ, provides the basis for openness between

Christians. The openness that was taught and practised by Jesus challenges us to move beyond a normal loving of those who love us to a radical loving of our enemy. Similarly, it would be normal for God to punish those who sin against God, but through God's radical openness, we are loved in spite of the things we do wrong.

Being open even towards our friends can sometimes be difficult for us, but being radically open to the other is something to which we are called in the Christian life. Jesus remains the best example for us to follow. What kind of things did Jesus do? Making light of every boundary and border – social, cultural, mental or religious – Jesus questioned, challenged and took the initiative. Notably, as the Messiah, he was not defined by Jewish expectations of the Messiah at all!

Jesus initiated conversations with those with whom his own people did not have good relationship. He was able to integrate and accommodate Gentiles and sinners, although that did not go down well, even sometimes among his own disciples. He entered into spaces that were clearly marked as hostile and he allowed those who were outside 'accepted' boundaries to enter into his space and welcomed them without hesitation.

Jesus invites us, his followers, to be radical when it comes to our attitudes towards the other: 'Do to others as you would have them do to you' (Luke 6.31). We do not do to others as they do to us, but as we want others to do to us, so we do to them. It is very simple and often very difficult, but it is possible for us to follow Jesus' example. Yet we don't want to forgive others, although we would like them to forgive us. We want selflessness in others while we struggle not to be selfish ourselves.

This chapter has seven studies on radical openness and the breaking of boundaries, both of which are essential for reconciliation and the building of relationships. In a hostile situation, Jesus proactively moves to the territory of the Samaritans and initiates a conversation with a Samaritan woman. In the context of a broken relationship, he initiates a conversation with Peter in order to restore him after his betrayal of Jesus. The parable of the labourers in the vineyard reminds us that we need to be radically open to the needs of others, especially when most contemporary conflicts are rooted in our greed to access resources at others' expense. We read of Peter's initial hesitation before he breaks through boundaries to go to the house of Cornelius to preach about Christ: such radical openness has a lot to teach us about how Christianity relates to other religions today. The parable of the 'prodigal son' reminds us that being radically open towards the other means not distancing ourselves from our own families or immediate communities. Ruth exhibits radical openness when she decides to go with her mother in law, knowing that she is making herself vulnerable by migrating to an unknown country where she will face many challenges. And when the disciples of Jesus have defined who is and who is not one of them, Jesus invites them to break their boundaries and to embrace the other who is outside. It is very soothing and comfortable for us to think that God is always on our side, but for reconciliation to work, we need to teach ourselves to also see God on the other side.

27 Initiating reconciliation in hostile contexts

Key text: John 4, 21
- Jesus and the Samaritan woman
- Jesus and Peter

It is an obvious fact that Jesus' ministry was always in the context of conflict, whether in response to those who were hostile or violent, or through mediating in interpersonal broken relationships between individuals. While God-human alienation was the primary reason for his incarnation, the first century world in which he lived and worked displayed many divisions among human beings. Jesus was part of a community that was hostile towards other communities – the Romans, the Samaritans and the Gentiles. It also had many internal conflicts and divisions, with contempt being shown towards the poor, sinners, lepers, women, the disabled and so on. Jesus, in one way or another, became part of the conflicting group, even though his will was always to bring together those who were divided. At times, when he witnessed conflict among his own disciples, he had to intervene and teach them how to live peaceably with one another. Sometimes the disciples' relationships with Jesus were also broken, notably when they betrayed and abandoned him.

Jesus' ministry is defined by his willingness to be proactive in breaking boundaries and moving into hostile territory to initiate reconciliation and set relationships right. In contrast, we as human beings have a tendency not to speak with one another when we are in conflict. This is usually our initial response. At the political and community level, not speaking or listening to one another is played out by leaders and representatives cancelling meetings as a mark of their unwillingness to reconcile. Indeed, many nations today struggle to converse with one another in a healthy way. Yet in many circumstances, as Jesus reminds us, conversation is the beginning of reconciliation.

In this study I would like to consider two incidents in the Bible where Jesus proactively breaks barriers to improve relations. The first is Jesus' conversation with the Samaritan woman whose community was in conflict with Jesus' community, and the second is Jesus' conversation with Peter after he betrayed his Lord.

The conflict between the Jews and the Samaritans was centuries old, dating back to the division of the kingdom into the south (Judah) and the north (Israel) after the rule of Solomon. Relationships became worse after the Israelites were captured by the Assyrians, diffused among other nations and forced to mix with the Gentiles. One of the consequences of this was that the Jews in the south wanted to keep them out during the reconstruction that took place at the time of Ezra and Nehemiah. Problems continued during Jesus' day, and he made several efforts to relate with the Samaritans. The conversation with the woman at the well is one.

In John 4, we see that Jesus deliberately enters into the territory of Samaria, although he could have well avoided it. At that time, if the Jews had to travel between Judea and Galilee, they would choose to take a longer route rather than pass through Samaria, which was in between these two territories. Jesus enters, arrives at the city of Sychar, and sits near a well, which is identified as Jacob's well. There he initiates a conversation with a Samaritan woman who comes to draw water. The repentance of this Samaritan woman, and the salvation that comes to her and the people in her village, constitute the ultimate end of the story. However, the reconciliation that takes place here must not be overlooked. Entering a hostile territory, in which he is not welcome, and initiating a conversation with a group of people his community dislikes, is not an easy or a pleasant task. Yet Jesus begins a process that leads to the salvation of many.

Similarly, Peter finds himself in a broken relationship with Jesus after he betrays him three times (Mark 14.66–72). Following the resurrection, Peter comes across Jesus on a few occasions, but is not willing to have a face-to-face meeting or a conversation. The most vocal of Jesus' disciples during his ministry runs away from him after his resurrection. When he realizes it is Jesus on the sea (John 21.7), Peter promptly jumps in, we assume, to get away. After this, when the disciples and Jesus meet, we still don't see any conversation between Peter and Jesus. In a group of more than 10 he tries to conceal himself, but when the time comes, Jesus initiates the much needed conversation; it is Jesus, the one betrayed by Peter, who makes the first move towards their reconciliation.

Through his conversations with the Samaritan woman and with Peter, Jesus teaches us that those on the powerful side need to show openness towards those on the other side in a conflict, if the reconciliation process is to become effective. Compared to the

Samaritan woman, Jesus is part of a dominant community – hostility between the Jews and the Samaritans was mutual, but the Jews were more passionate about despising the Samaritans and considering them inferior. Similarly, as the resurrected Lord, Jesus is in the commanding position when he invites Peter to talk. It is apt that Jesus starts the conversation.

Both in intergroup and in interpersonal conflicts, a major stumbling block for us is the initiating of a conversation. Most of the time, ego, enmity and hostility stand in the way (as for the Samaritan woman) or fear, guilt and shame (as for Peter). Even when we are open to the idea of being reconciled, we hesitate to take the first step of going to talk to the person involved.

Of course, in the complex context of conflict today, everyone thinks they are a victim in one way or other. Some powerful nations, who once plundered poor countries of the world (and may continue to do so), are convinced they are the ones who are suffering due to migration, global economic policies and other factors. In interpersonal conflicts, it's easy to believe that we are the wronged one and that the other should attempt to make restitution with us for what they have done. Jesus, though, in spite of being on the powerful side, takes the initiative in seeking reconciliation.

Once a conversation is begun, however, it is a major challenge to keep it going, as the other party may be keen to shut it down. On a few occasions, the Samaritan woman seems to try to do this. Her questions to Jesus could be construed as quite hostile and irritating: 'How is it that you, a Jew, ask a drink of me, a woman of Samaria?' (verse 9), and 'Are you greater than our ancestor Jacob?' (verse 12). Yet Jesus perseveres. Of course, later in the story the woman slowly engages with Jesus and asks more probing questions, anticipating answers she can start to apply to her life. This is the longest (recorded) uninterrupted conversation Jesus has with one individual. There are thirteen dialogues in the thread, which is quite significant given the context.

Unlike the Samaritan woman, Peter does not try to bring a halt to his conversation with Jesus, but Jesus repeats the question 'do you love me?' three times, in spite of Peter answering him in the affirmative. It seems that Jesus wants Peter to fully comprehend his betrayal without talking about the betrayal itself. Of course, by avoiding facing Jesus, Peter reveals how guilty he feels at what he did, but Jesus seems keen to really press the matter home. This second conversation, in which a broken relationship is set right once and for all, is as unique as the first.

In the world today, we have begun to realize that the quality of our communication is not what it once was. Stephen Miller's *Conversation: A History of a Declining Art* captures this situation very well. Even while information technology and communication systems are progressing to an advanced stage, communication between human beings is shrinking. People do get in touch with one another through different means, but personal and group level face-to-face conversations are becoming fewer. Many people are content with gadgets, with a focus on their own pleasure. This is worrying because it is of the utmost importance for the future of humanity that we focus on mending broken relationships and building new ones.

Among nations today, the availability of weapons, the will and the power to dominate, having enough economic resources, and what is often seen as 'self-sufficiency', mean that conversation is considered useless. We are slowly but dangerously moving towards unilateral relationships. Even though some heads and representatives of governments appear to support international dialogue, we suspect they despise their conversation partners in secret.

It is only through conversation that we shall learn to understand the roots of a problem and become convinced of the need for solutions. Conversations challenge fixations and established prejudices. The Samaritan woman asks Jesus how a Jew can ask her for water, but in the end, both her binary thinking and her hostility are overcome and she is able to relate to Jesus and become a witness to her neighbours in her village. Jesus, the Samaritan woman and Peter were dealing with pain, wounds, guilt, shame and the hostility of wider communities in their conversations. It is beginning those conversations that is the crucial thing, and Jesus models how to break through barriers so that we can talk to one another and move towards greater understanding.

Questions for reflection

1 What are some of the obstacles we face when we want to initiate a conversation to reconcile with someone?
2 Reflect on an occasion when you struggled to sort out a broken relationship through conversation or were successful in doing so.
3 Jesus teaches us that the one on the powerful side should initiate the conversation. Why is this important?

28 A lesson in radical openness

Key text: Matthew 20.1–16
The parable of the labourers in the vineyard

The unequal distribution of resources remains one of the main reasons for conflict and violence in our world today, with a few powerful people, communities and nations prospering vastly at the expense of poorer disadvantaged ones. The creation of more wealth due to scientific advancement has not changed the situation, only widened the gap between rich and poor. Bringing about reconciliation in such a context is not easy, because it does not involve simply breaking down barriers; it requires the rich and powerful to be willing to share their resources and privileges, and commit to justice and equality if reconciliation is to be successful and peace to prevail. Blaming the poor for being poor is not helpful, and justifying a few people's right to own and use most of the earth's resources is not just. Indeed, addressing the question of economic justice is key, and essential to this is showing a radical openness to others and their needs (i.e. those who are poor and disadvantaged compared to ourselves) so the process of reconciliation may begin.

Jesus' parable of the labourers in the vineyard is one of a number of parables he tells about how the Kingdom of God functions. In this story, the labourers join the work in the vineyard at different points in the day, but all end at the same time. Surprisingly, everyone gets the same pay – those who have worked only one hour and those who have toiled for several. One of Jesus' main aims in the parable is to explain how sinners and those rejected by society will advance in the Kingdom of God, while those who think the Kingdom is theirs will be left behind.

The events of the story are not what we might call normal. From what we would think of as a natural justice perspective, what the landowner does seems ridiculous and unacceptable. Our general understanding is that those who labour more should receive more and those who labour less should receive less; otherwise, we encourage laziness and inequality among those who do not work and discourage those who work hard. Our everyday life and ethics would make it difficult for us to act as Jesus suggests here.

Yet this parable is not simply about being rewarded for work, or 'the last will be first and the first will be last'. Among other things, we see openness and generosity in the landowner toward the labourers, particularly the latecomers. We also see hard feelings among those who came early, as they struggle to accept that the landowner is paying the latecomers more than their due – and what seems, in a way, to be more than they are receiving themselves. Although it is the landowner who appears to have created conditions of unhappiness, it is those who came early who find themselves in conflict.

The only way they can reconcile themselves with what is happening is by appreciating the generosity of the owner, who is as concerned for the latecomers as he is for them. The owner, without doing any injustice to those who came early, invites them, through his 'abnormal' act, to learn a lesson in radical openness to the needs of the other.

When we look at the attitudes of those who came early, we find that the presence of others becomes a problem for them. What would have happened if those who came late had not come at all? The early workers would have gone home happily with the wage they received, which had been agreed between them and the owner at the start of the day. The parable reveals how the proximity and welfare of others often becomes an issue leading to conflict. Perhaps it is part of the owner's plan, as he teaches about openness toward the other, to make their presence a necessity.

Second, those who came early expected more than was due to them. Many biblical scholars believe that one day's wage was normally what was required for the living expenses of an average family for a day. Those who came early did indeed bear 'the burden of the day and the scorching heat', as a natural part of their agreement with the owner. Yet when they see those who began work later receiving the same wage that they themselves require and have agreed, they expect more. They are not pleased, complaining 'These last worked only one hour, and you have made them equal to us' (verse 12). Struggling for equality is a challenge for the disadvantaged. But here those who are already in a better position complain about others being *made equal* to them, which shows they assume others are inferior.

Third, we need to look at the context of the latecomers joining the work. They are found in the streets. It is the owner who goes out again and again looking for workers for the vineyard. The fact that there are those who are willing to work for only one hour shows how desperate they are to earn something for the day. Some of the latecomers tell the owner, when he asks why are they standing on the road, that no one has hired them (verse 7). Even at the 'eleventh hour' they are eagerly waiting for work. Obviously, they are not lazy; it is more a question of opportunity. They did not manage to secure work, unlike those who were hired early in the day.

Those hired early fail to recognize the latecomers' needs, however, in spite of the latter's desperate longing to be hired. The early workers seem unable to imagine themselves in a similar position. How frantic would they have been if they had shared the latecomers' experience? Having been hired, starting work so late in the day would bring worries of how much the owner might give them. No, the early workers think only of themselves, feel aggrieved that they are badly off although they are working for an assured wage, and are unable to recognize the pain and difficulty of those who were waiting on the streets for the opportunity to earn even one hour's pay. The latecomers do not really take anything from the early workers – they are simply the beneficiaries of the owner's generosity.

Finally, the landowner, who is the embodiment of openness, wants to teach a lesson in radical openness to those who came early, who thought they had a right to more. In spite of the attitude of those who came early, the landowner is kind and open towards all the workers he sends to his vineyard. He is personally involved in finding and hiring his labourers, leaving early in the morning to do so, and going out again and again. He *engages* with the labourers on their wages. He is happy to 'agree' with them the usual daily sum. He does not negotiate to reduce it! His concern is not only with his vineyard, but also with people and their needs. That is why he goes to the streets again and again, even at the eleventh hour. He *might* need more workers; but he is *aware* that more workers – desperate to make a living – are available, and he feels compelled to seek and find them. When he sends the labourers late on, he agrees to pay 'whatever is right', and may already have in mind to give what they require for their living expenses for the day.

He commands his manager to pay the workers, beginning with those who came late and to give an equal amount to everyone. Here the owner seems determined to teach the workers a lesson. He could easily have paid the early ones first, and they would have gone away happy with what they were due; but he switches the order. He wants those who came early to *know* what he is giving the latecomers. It is an encouragement to us to be radically open towards the other – their circumstances, their pain and their needs.

This is a difficult lesson to learn. We find it easy to approve what happens in this parable, yet it is not at all easy for us to follow what the owner does. As the disciples questioned Jesus, so we may ask 'it is possible for whom?' (Matthew 19.25). Indeed, it is possible for God, and Jesus here gives us a lesson in radical openness that we are invited to follow.

In our capitalist society, employers are often in conflict with labourers, and it is very difficult to find people who own resources (who are often convinced of their 'right to more') to be radically open to the needs of others. In the normal way of things, it just doesn't happen. In Jesus' Kingdom, however, this is the way things work! The reconciliation ministry he has initiated and given to us to follow in our Christian life will not be fruitful without an attitude of radical openness.

In South India, where I come from and have lived most of my life, I used to be amazed at the take up of one particular occupation among the not formally educated families: Palmyra climbing (although this is unfortunately now disappearing for various reasons). Palmyra climbing is a difficult job involving hard labour, because the trees are about 25–30 metres tall, but the juice the tree produces is natural and healthy; before cane sugar began to be used instead, the work was quite popular. While the men climbed the trees and brought the juice down, the women in the house would make jaggery (boiling the juice until it becomes solid means it lasts for days without any preservative) – although some made toddy (liquor), which in fact caused huge socio-economic problems for poor families. Those who climb the trees are labourers who work with the owners of a few Palmyras, but what is very interesting and, indeed, surprising is that in this work (and in none other I know of), the profit is equally divided between the owner of the trees and the labourers. When the juice is brought down, each gets an equal share. This is really radical and, along with other researchers, I am still trying to discover how such a fair system came to be put in place.

Questions for reflection

1   When God calls us from our normal lives to do something radical, how do we respond?

2 Why is a radical openness to others and their needs essential for an effective reconciliation ministry?

3 How can we overcome comparative attitudes with those who are poorer and more disadvantaged than us in order to justify our 'right to more'?

29 Peter and Cornelius

Key text: Acts 10
Peter's openness to the Gentiles

A case of radical openness among the first disciples of Jesus can be seen in the ministry of Peter the Apostle. This case is vividly depicted in Acts 10, when Peter is invited to broaden his understanding of God and of God's dealings with others. For although the disciples often witnessed Jesus breaking boundaries to embrace and reconcile people, they struggled when the same was asked of them (unsurprisingly perhaps, given the conflicts they had among themselves). Even after Jesus' resurrection, they did not find this easy. Nonetheless, they were repeatedly invited to understand that God is God of all and that God is at work in the lives of other people, even though we may not be aware of it.

Christians throughout the world, particularly in the West, continue to struggle to relate to people of other faiths, with attitudes towards truth, salvation and mission influencing our thinking. Although Acts 10 is not about Christians relating to non-Christians, rather about a Jew breaking boundaries to reach and relate to Gentiles with the message of Christ (verse 36), it has lessons for us regarding how we co-exist harmoniously with those of other religions.

The most important thing about the Peter-Cornelius encounter is that Peter learns more from it than Cornelius! Although it is Cornelius, prompted by an angel of God, who wants Peter to tell him more about God revealed in Christ, in the end, it is the vision granted to Peter that becomes both a turning point and a crucial lesson to the first disciples on showing greater openness to those who belong to different groups.

First, we see there is a struggle in Peter as he refuses – not once but three times – to eat what comes to him from heaven. Then, after expressing his initial reservations, he listens to God and accepts that he should not call anyone profane or unclean. He eventually understands that he needs to overthrow the established way of thinking – that the Jews are sacred and the Gentiles profane. He honestly acknowledges this struggle to Cornelius (verse 28), telling him that God has shown him that what God has made clean, he must not call profane.

Second, listening to God, Peter breaks the law. I do not mean a law that exists for the well-being of a community, but one concerned with constructing walls and boundaries between people, based on their social, cultural or ethnic differences. The law Peter breaks is one that includes some and excludes many and is built on hate for those who are different. This is not only a good breaking of the law, it is a necessary one too. Peter gradually comes to realize that a law that keeps some in and some out on spurious grounds cannot be ordained by God.

Third, through his encounter with Cornelius, Peter's understanding of God widens. When Cornelius says that God spoke to him, Peter realizes and admits that God shows no partiality, but accepts anyone who fears him and does what is right and acceptable (verses 34–35). Thus, someone whom Peter considered profane and unclean and who he was forbidden to visit, influences his comprehension of God. Through Cornelius, Peter understands God better and becomes a radically open person. It is because of this change in him that he says to Cornelius, when the latter falls on his feet, 'Stand up, I am only a mortal' (verse 26). When we overcome boundaries, we begin to know who we are and where we belong.

Cornelius plays an important part in helping Peter understand that God is at work in other nations (and other religions' traditions in today's terms), and that God is impartial. Fearing God, alms-giving and prayers to God – these three things are repeatedly mentioned as explaining how and why Cornelius has been accepted by God. Other things will follow, of course, but the relationship has been established.

It is a very difficult lesson for many Christians today to understand how God can regard things as clean that we think unclean. Looking at verse 35, we may also have a particular problem with the word 'anyone' because it challenges our assumed special status, our chosenness. God's 'anyone' makes it clear that, while we may want to build boundaries, God actually breaks them and wants us to break them.

Finally, Peter's experience with Cornelius reveals that God or the Holy Spirit (verses 44–48) is not bound by our conception of mission. Jesus shows this again and again. This story is not simply about opening up mission to the Gentiles (as it is often understood to be), but about how the mission to the Gentiles helps Peter and the other Apostles understand God better and become open to others by listening to God. Peter is reminded that God has God's way of working, with or without the involvement of the disciples. If the mission belongs to God, we are only participants in it, and God works in a number of ways *unknown* to us. It takes some time for Peter to learn this lesson, but in our current context, we continue to struggle with a truth Peter and other Apostles took on board centuries ago.

Of course, all of this only galvanizes Peter further in bearing witness to what God has done in Christ. There is no disharmony between what God has been doing among the Gentiles, and what God has been doing through Jesus Christ, specifically among the Jews. Now the knowledge of God's work through Jesus Christ draws the Gentiles closer to God.

Peter learns a lesson in radical openness to others in also accepting that God is active in other traditions. It was a dose of training he needed, as did the other disciples. Today, we too are challenged to overcome our negative attitudes with regard to our neighbours from different faiths. Remember, radical openness is not something that *undermines* God, but something God wants us to have when we relate to people of other faiths and no faith.

Questions for reflection

1 In spite of our belief that God is God of all and that we have all been created in the image of God, it seems difficult for us to develop good relationships with people of other religions and no religion. Why do you think this might be?

2 Reflect on one or two major aspects about our belief in God that affect our relationships with people of other religions and traditions.

3 What are some of the efforts your local church or community make in building relationships with people from other religions? How might they be taken further?

30 The lost son who distanced himself from his own

Key text: Luke 15
The parable of 'the prodigal son'

While an open attitude towards others and a willingness to break boundaries are crucial in the reconciliation process, we may often find that we distance ourselves from people close to us. Perhaps we have an individual, possibly selfish, ambition that is not met: how easy to detach from our family, community, congregation or local group in protest. Similarly, problems over minor issues can lead those in local congregations to distance themselves from one another. How this kind of behaviour affects the process of reconciliation is revealed in Luke 15.

Of course, it is obvious that the basic purpose of Luke 15 is to expose the unhappiness of those who were unwilling to accept all those who come to Jesus Christ. As we see in verses 1 and 2, the Pharisees and the scribes are grumbling at the tax collectors and sinners gathering to hear him. This leads Jesus to tell three parables, those of the lost sheep, the lost coin and the lost son. The basic theme of all three is the divine imperative to respond to the recovery of the lost with joy. The third parable stands out because it refers to those who do not want to celebrate in such a way (who are not explicitly mentioned in the first two).

What Jesus tried to convey in these stories to the self-righteous Pharisees and scribes, who regarded themselves favourably compared to sinners, was significant in terms of mission during Jesus' time, as it still is in ours today. While the first two parables talk about the loss and restoration of material possessions, the third speaks of personal relationships between a father, his elder son and the son's younger brother. The elder son finds himself expected to participate in joy and celebration when his brother returns home; what he actually does is to distance himself in several ways.

First, the elder brother distances himself from himself. As we read in verse 25, he is returning home, but stops on the way when he hears sounds of music and dancing, which suggest something celebratory is going on. It is surely not necessary for the son to call a slave and ask about this – if you hear joyful sounds coming from your own home, do you not hurry there and join the celebration? Yet the son dissociates from what is happening even before he knows the reason for it. It appears that he does not want to participate in other people's happiness. Their happiness causes unhappiness in him, which seems to suggest a kind of perverse mentality and a distancing from himself.

When the elder son discovers that his younger brother's return is the reason for joy and celebration, he becomes furious and refuses to go into the house. Anger is a natural human emotion, but it can be one of the factors leading to abnormal behaviour. Anger can cause us to lose touch with our normal self. To be so angry that you decline to enter your own house could suggest a personality problem. The elder son is a refuser of festivities, a churl, a personality similar to others we see in the Bible, such as Jonah or some of the Pharisees. A refuser of festivities is motivated by personal interest. Choosing not to participate in the joyful activities of the community and thus detaching yourself from others' happiness – happiness that makes even the heavens sing – may be equated with refusing to participate in God's salvation. The elder son thus distances himself from God's redeeming activity.

Another sign of distancing from his own self becomes evident when we note what the elder son says to his father. He tells him that he has been working like a servant for him all these years and has never disobeyed his command. At first this looks like a positive statement. It is expected of a son to be humble and obedient, but note the self-righteousness coming through. The elder son is taking pride in humility, which is a very dangerous act indeed! He feels he deserves something for all he has given, which puts him in the group of those who feel that they are not treated as well as they deserve. He sees himself as the model son, but ironically, he equates himself with a slave.

Second, we see that the elder son distances himself from his father. Verse 28 says that the father pleads with him to go into the house, but he refuses. The way in which he speaks to his father is certainly disrespectful in the context in which this parable was told. He does not address him as 'Father', but starts his conversation with the word 'listen' or 'look'. Somewhat arrogant, and a punishable offence in Old Testament terms as the honouring of parents is expected of children. We might contrast the elder brother's address with the way in which his younger brother speaks to his father in verse 21.

Not only does the elder son disrespect his father, he also accuses him: 'you have never given me even a young goat, but you have given a fatted calf for your son.' It appears that the elder son simply does not understand his own father. In spite of being at home with him, he seems to have lived in alienation from him. The elder son is blind to the fact that the father feels he has lavished the same care and concern on him that he is extending to his younger brother. The outburst that his father has never given a goat is accusation without understanding!

The elder son also distances himself from his father by comparing himself with his brother. When doing so, he forgets entirely what he has already secured. He does not realize that whatever the Father has belongs to him as well. This kind of thing can happen in our lives too. When we compare ourselves with others, it is easy to forget or ignore the blessings God has already given us. Suddenly all we have becomes secondary or insignificant. Instead of being thankful to God for God's blessings, we distance ourselves from God.

Third, let us look now at how the elder son distances himself from his brother. In verse 30, speaking to his father, the elder one calls his brother 'this son of yours'. His hate is such that he is denying their relationship. He does not want to acknowledge that the person who has repented and returned is his own brother. The younger brother is just a good-for-nothing to him. The irony is that, by his behaviour, it is the elder brother who has become the lost son.

Perhaps he fears that what has been allotted to him may be divided again for the sake of his younger brother. Of course, the elder brother's concern for justice is natural, but the father's attitude is that what was lost has been found. He is not bothered about material possessions – sharing or not sharing them. They don't matter. For him, joy has come again because his son has repented and his return is to be celebrated. That is all.

In the process of distancing himself from his younger brother, the elder one contrasts his own friends with his brother's 'prostitutes'. He makes no effort to understand the friendlessness of his brother, which might have been what led the younger son to come to appreciate his father's love, but talks about his own friends in a positive light. He seems to be judgmental here, assuming he knows what kind of life his younger brother would have lived when he was away. The parable does not reveal whether what he thinks is so; neither do we know why he makes such accusations. What is clear is that he wants to put down and demonize his brother, and he does this in spite of knowing that his father has already forgiven and accepted him.

We can see that the more the elder brother distances himself, the more his father asserts that he loves him as he loves his younger son. He pleads with the elder brother to enter into his home, assures him that it his own house, tenderly calls him 'son' and emphasizes again in verse 32 that the younger one is 'this brother of yours'.

The parable of the lost son is mainly about a lost or prodigal son rising because of his repentance, and another son falling because he fails in his relationships – he distances himself from his own self, from his father and from his brother. Susan Ertz, an English writer and author of the book *The Prodigal Heart*, says that: 'while the younger was prodigal in body, at least part of his heart was always at home.' We can assume that is why, when he was in distress, he was able to think of his home, his father and his father's servants. 'But the elder brother was prodigal at heart and only his body was at home.'

Questions for reflection

1 Think of times when you have taken pride in your humility like the elder son. Have you become unhappy about others' happiness? Have you lost sight of God's blessings as you compare yourselves with others?

2 In what ways do we distance ourselves from our own normal self (which has been created by God and which is in God's image), from God and from our neighbours?

3 How might a lack of radical openness be as dangerous as distancing from others in the context of conflict and reconciliation?

31 Ruth: 'Your people are my people'

Key text: Ruth 1
Ruth and Naomi

In the context of building relationships with people of other cultures, Ruth is an interesting and much-loved biblical character. When our instinct is to segregate ourselves from those who are different from us, her words 'your people are my people' (verse 16) both challenge and inspire us. It would not be easy for Ruth to utter these powerful words given the circumstances in which she finds herself. Yet her willingness to be ready to move with her mother-in-law Naomi, wherever she would go, result in Ruth becoming an important figure in the genealogy of Jesus.

Although named Ruth, the story in this book of the Bible is told from the Israelite community's point of view. Ruth has an important role to play, but unlike Esther, she is not presented as a heroine. Rather, she lives as one who is under the shadow of first Naomi and later Boaz. The opening chapter is more about the suffering of Naomi, who has lost both her husband and her sons, than about Ruth. Later Ruth behaves like an obedient daughter-in-law in seeking the favour of Boaz (note that in Judah her foreign identity, as a Moabite, is constantly referred to). However, Ruth exhibits a radical openness to the other such as we rarely see among human beings, and hers is not a story of reconciliation in the sense of mending broken relationships, but surely in terms of being open to the other and willing to build relationships with the other. The story offers a number of insights relevant to our contemporary context, in which migration and the coming together of cultures have become contested issues.

1 Ruth's radical openness to the other enables her to identify with the vulnerability of Naomi

Ruth fully understands and sympathizes with Naomi's situation. Naomi feels wretched and openly expresses this again and again. She is in a foreign land. Her husband is dead. Her two sons are dead. The famine is cruel. She has lost everything. It is all hopeless. She cannot anticipate things will ever get any better, but expects only more suffering, even as she plans to return home to Judah after several years in Moab. When she gets back, she asks her people to call her

Mara (verse 20), as 'Bitter' sums up everything she is now. But Naomi *is* concerned that her daughters-in-law are safe and settled. One of them, Oprah, obviously agreeing with Naomi that she will be better off anywhere else than with her, chooses to go back to her parents' place.

Ruth, however, is determined to stick with her mother-in-law and to be with her wherever she goes. Her stubbornness in the light of Naomi's wretchedness suggests Ruth is radically open to identifying and showing solidarity with the vulnerable. She surely knows that Naomi will be a burden for her because of her old age, but as the younger woman she is willing to take on that responsibility. Her words to Naomi are deeply moving:

> 'Do not press me to leave you
>   or to turn back from following you!
> Where you go, I will go;
>   where you lodge, I will lodge;
> your people shall be my people,
>   and your God my God.
> Where you die, I will die—
>   there will I be buried.
> May the Lord do thus and so to me,
>   and more as well,
> if even death parts me from you!'   (Ruth 1.16–17)

Ruth implores her mother-in-law not to try to persuade her to abandon her. The way in which she expresses her solidarity with Naomi has the overtones of a covenant: the words 'May the LORD do thus and so to me, and more as well' (verse 17) would normally be used in covenants between kings or community leaders. This means they are not mere words. By bringing God into her commitment to be with Naomi, Ruth expresses her resolve never to leave her.

Why does Ruth make this decision? What prompts her to identify so strongly with a person like Naomi who is in an extremely vulnerable position? We don't know. However, the way Ruth acts has much to teach us about Christian living and our attitudes towards the other.

2 Ruth's radical openness makes herself vulnerable

To identify with Naomi's vulnerability, Ruth has to leave where she belongs, knowing that this will also make her vulnerable.

Ruth realizes that Naomi cannot produce another son for her to marry. She may need to forget about having a husband at all and live as a widow forever. She has absolutely no idea what her future is going to be – her mother-in-law, who is already in a vulnerable and wretched condition, is her only hope.

Ruth also leaves behind relative security. The fact that Oprah decides to return to Moab indicates that there is still a chance of life there, but Ruth decides to move out of her comfort zone for the sake of Naomi.

As we have the benefit of knowing how everything turns out, we are aware that Ruth's fortunes are going to improve dramatically. However, when she makes her decision, things could not look more unpromising. In planning to leave her own country, Ruth becomes even more vulnerable than Naomi. After all, she too has lost her husband. Now, in addition to meeting her needs, she also has to care for Naomi.

3   Ruth's radical openness will put her at risk in a new country

Naomi, her husband and sons originally moved from Judah to Moab, so Ruth is already part of a migrant family and knows the difficulties associated with migration. Now, because she is willing to be with Naomi, she has to move to a completely unfamiliar country and adapt to a new culture, new people and a new environment. As the only person she knows in Judah is the vulnerable Naomi, she will need to depend on the generosity and hospitality of others, to whom she is a complete stranger.

Ruth's identity in this foreign land will be uncertain. She is taking a risk moving to a country that does not generally have a good relationship with her own. Moab is often despised in the Old Testament, mainly because the king of Moab, Balak, persuaded Balaam to curse Israel when they were journeying from Egypt to the Promised Land. Ruth may be treated with suspicion and possibly assumed to be a spy and a threat to the nation. She could be vulnerable to judgement, rejection and even violence.

As the story goes on, we learn that Ruth is not, in fact, welcomed (initially at least) into the Israelite community. Her loyalty is continuously suspect, and we hear her called a Moabite again and again. She has to work hard to be accepted and integrated, yet she voluntarily stepped into this situation when she decided to go with her mother-in-law. Later Ruth shows even greater character and integrity when she obeys Naomi to go to meet Boaz.

Today, migration tends to be opposed. We think of it largely in terms of countries who receive migrants and countries who do not want to welcome them. However, Ruth's story reminds us that migrating can be more challenging for the migrants than for the countries who accept them.

We often talk about the need for receptivity towards migrants, refugees and foreigners. What may be ignored is the fact that it takes a lot of faith on their part to move to other countries. Relating migration to economic aspiration can blind us to the everyday struggles people have. When powerful nations in the world and well-off communities in a local context in many countries are struggling to welcome migrants, Ruth's story tells of the extraordinary openness a migrant shows towards the country she moves to and of how she affects the welfare of the people there. This is a woman who migrates in order to save God's people. A non-Israelite's move into Israel is critical for the well-being of Israel!

Ruth's story may appear to be about her accommodation into the Israelite community, but it is actually Ruth who accommodates Naomi and the Israelite community into her own life, by identifying with the vulnerable, becoming vulnerable herself and then deliberately moving towards uncertainty. She relates to something that is not her own. She accepts the other as her own. As we attempt to mend broken relationships and create new relationships with the other – something that is vital to the future well-being of humanity – Ruth continues to challenge us through her radical openness to the other.

Questions for reflection

1 When someone is in a state of utter wretchedness, what makes us identify with them? How can we cultivate compassion?
2 Radical openness involves risk-taking. Can you think of how this impacts on your own life?
3 As a local congregation or community, what simple steps can we take to welcome migrants?

32 Becoming friends: Jesus' way

Key text: Luke 9.49-50
The exorcist who was not with the disciples

> John answered, 'Master, we saw someone casting out demons in your name, and we tried to stop him, because he does not follow with us.' But Jesus said to him, 'Do not stop him; for whoever is not against you is for you.'

Lack of openness towards the other is something Jesus' disciples often show despite spending so long by his side. Jesus often has to shock them into realizing that they are connected with others rather than detached – after all, unity is a requirement of the Kingdom of God!

Luke 9.49–50, which has a parallel in Mark 9.38–40, is one of many conversations between Jesus and the disciples, and the context here is that some of the disciples' failures have been exposed. In the preceding passages, Jesus rebukes them for not being able to cast out demons (37–43), and for fighting among themselves about who is greatest among them (46–48). Furthermore, they have failed to understand Jesus' words about his death (44–45). So it is hardly surprising that John brings up the issue of an unnamed man casting out demons. To their chagrin, Jesus provides an answer the disciples probably did not expect, and thus once again exposes their lack of understanding about how Christian disciples should relate to one another.

Jesus' words, 'Do not stop him, for whoever is not against you is for you' are not simply an instruction: they are also an invitation to openness. Jesus tells the disciples not to worry about those who are not opposing them, and this has implications for what they *should* be doing. They have created boundaries and Jesus is concerned that they overcome these and build relationships with others. This passage may not be overtly about friendship or reconciliation, but it definitely offers pointers on both of these things – for the disciples of Jesus then and for us now.

1 Do not set parameters for others in Christian discipleship

The disciples of Jesus assume that the unnamed man is against them because he is not with them or not like them – meaning he is not in their group. They perceive reality according to the parameters and boundaries they themselves set, and think their rules determine who can or cannot be a part of Jesus' ministry. Even though the man is healing in Jesus' name, that is not sufficient for the disciples. He is different and so constitutes someone in opposition to them. They are constructing boundaries and creating stereotypes based on their perceptions.

Jesus does not want his disciples to do this. He encourages them to change their thinking, beginning with an understanding of who is not their enemy. He wants them to accommodate the unnamed exorcist and what he was doing, rather than talk about whether or not he belongs in their camp. We see in the passage just before this one, the disciples have been unable to cast out demons, unlike this man who does so very successfully (verses 40–41). The disciples are invited to see themselves as part of the wider ministry of God, rather than exercising their (presumed) authority to include and exclude others and thus keep themselves at the centre of power.

2 Do not define who your friends are – look for who is not your enemy

The disciples were looking for 'who was with us', yet Jesus tells them to look for those who may not be with them, but who are not against them.

According to the principle Jesus sets out here, we too are invited to look for 'who is not our enemy' or 'who is not against us', rather than looking to see who are our friends. We have to start with those 'who are not against us'.

The historical background to this saying suggests it was a kind of proverb in use among the Greeks and Romans. Here it makes an appearance in Roman politics:

> Cicero tells the Caesar thus: 'Though we held all to be our opponents but [except] those on our side, you [Caesar] counted all as your adherents who were not against you.' (*Pro Quintino Ligario* 33). Or, '… while we considered all who were not with us as our enemies, you considered all who were not against you as your friends.'
>
> (*Pro Quintino Ligario* 33)

This kind of thinking underpins how the political classes use enemies and friends to survive, even today. What is generally regarded as a political principle is thus employed by Jesus here to support his instruction to the disciples on how they should relate to other disciples.

The disciples have a particular idea of who is for them and who is against them, and their thinking is conventional – that is, whoever is not for them must be against them. Jesus asks that they think outside the box, as it were, and move their focus so they begin with the question of who is not against them. It is easy to decide who our friends are – that is clear and defined; it is much more difficult to pin down those people who are not against us – that is complex and vague. As always, Jesus invites his disciples to take the difficult path.

We may wonder how someone can be our friend if they are not 'with us'. To consider this is confusing, and we may be so concerned to reassure ourselves about the people who are with us, that we simply fail to give the other category much thought.

3 Become friends with one another rather than making friends

How can we gain a better understanding of this concept of one who is not with us but not against us? Jesus' answer implies that we simply have to start from ourselves. His understanding, unlike Caesar's, is that looking for 'who is not our enemy' is basically an invitation for us to become friends ourselves. We have to work out whether we are against someone or not! This means becoming a good friend rather than looking for good friends. Considering the question 'who is not against you' basically implies that changes are expected *in ourselves*, and that these will be important in the building of new relationships.

To put this in a slightly different way, what Jesus says here makes it clear that it is the disciples' responsibility – and ours – *to make sure that we are not an enemy to the other*. However, if we look for a friend who is not against us, our attitude will impact on that friend so they are more concerned to be a friend to us than to become our enemy. Thus, looking for 'who is not our enemy' helps us 'become' friends rather than 'make' friends.

In fact in this text it is the disciples of Jesus who find themselves against someone – the unnamed exorcist who they try to exclude from discipleship and from the ministry of Jesus. They are not asked to make the unnamed person their friend, but Jesus' words indicate that the disciples should find a way of *becoming* friends with him.

When we are concerned with *who is my friend, where is my friend,* responsibility is centred on our friends who have to make sure they are not bad friends to us. However, looking for who is not against us has greater implications. Our change in attitude is what will get the friendship going, and that is what Jesus' model aims to encourage.

The exercise of looking for who is not our enemy may make us feel self-critical and wonder why these people are not our friends. This can be an opportunity for us to own and correct our own mistakes – and to be open about these, which is an essential part of growing in relationship with one another. Today it has become a habit for powerful nations and communities to ask other nations and communities: Are you with us or against us? The idea is to look for friends to fight against common enemies.

Jesus is inviting us as his disciples to be radically open to the other – the one who is outside the boundary defined by us. He challenges us to break the boundaries we often create to exclude the other, sometimes even within Christian discipleship.

Questions for reflection

1 What circumstances prompt us to construct boundaries even though we are seeking to serve God through discipleship in Christ?
2 Jesus' disciples, in spite of being with him for so long, struggled to take on board his teaching about breaking boundaries. How has this study helped you in your own efforts to be radically open to the other?
3 Can you think of people who are not against you with whom you could become friends?

33 Learning to see God on the other side!

Key text: Luke 4.25–30
There are others in the plan and mission of God

Learning to see God on the other side is an important step in Christian reconciliation. The most radical of Jesus' teachings and actions brought him into constant confrontation with those who thought that God was on their side, only on their side and always on their side.

God on the other side

For centuries the Israelites had thought that God was always on their side. As we trace their journey of faith in the Old Testament, we see that the Israelites remembered God, and trusted that God was with them – and only with them – as God helped them fight their wars against the Egyptians, the Philistines and other peoples. On the positive side, such faith helped them to depend upon God for their livelihood and for protection, and empowered them when they faced oppression in Egypt or hostility from people around them. However, there were many times when their confidence in God being on their side led them to construct boundaries and exclude or exploit others – people of their own nation as well as of others. As a result, many of the vulnerable and disadvantaged were condemned. Yet we can see, even in the lives of the Israelites, that God in the Old Testament is God of all. There are countless examples of God being with others. And although the Israelites believed God fought their own battles, the same God also instructed them to live with their neighbours in peace and harmony.

When Sarah thinks God is with her by promising that she and Abraham will have a son, we see that God is also with Hagar (Sarah's Egyptian handmaid) and Ishmael (Abraham's son by her). God was not always on the side of Israelites. Often God expresses love and care towards their neighbours: 'You shall not abhor any of the Edomites, for they are your kin. You shall not abhor any of the Egyptians, because you were an alien residing in their land' (Deuteronomy 23.7). God is angry about Uriah's murder, arranged by David and carried out by proxy, when David thinks that God is with him by giving him the whole kingdom of Israel. God is on the side of the lepers through whom God saves the Israelites when they are in trouble (2 Kings 7). God is with the Babylonians, the Assyrians and others, even if this is so they may chastise the Israelites. God often uses people other than the Israelites for different purposes and in various ways. Jonah is unable to find God with the people of Nineveh, but God is on their side when they draw near to God!

Jesus on the other side

Jesus often finds himself on the other side (Matthew 8.18; Luke 8.22; Mark 5.21, 8.13). Going to the other side is a regular and routine activity in his ministry and is symbolic of the need to cross all kinds of boundaries – physical, social, cultural, economic and political. Jesus says to the disciples, 'Let us go across to the other side' (Mark 4.35), and asks them to 'try on the other side' (John 21.6).

Jesus regularly goes to the other side.

Jesus lives on the other side.

Jesus is with those on the other side.

Against the disciples' expectations, against the expectations of the Pharisees, the Scribes and other powerful people of Jesus' time, and against the expectations of the people around him, Jesus is always on the other side.

As we have seen in some studies in this book:

- The Pharisee thought that God was on his side, but God was actually on the side of the tax collector.
- Jesus is on the side of the unnamed exorcist, although the disciples thought Jesus was only on theirs.
- Jesus is on the side of the Samaritan village when the disciples want to curse it (Luke 9.51–56).
- Peter saw that God was on his side, but God was on the side of Cornelius too, accepting and appraising his prayers and giving him a vision. Peter actually had to go to the other side to see and realize God fully!

There are others in the plan and mission of God

In Luke 4.25–30, which is called the Nazareth Manifesto, Jesus clearly tells the people in the synagogue that they are not the only ones in the plan and mission of God, and that others can receive the blessings of God. Jesus begins by reading from Isaiah 61.1–3, a passage that

140

expresses God's liberation and comfort of the poor, the oppressed and the sick. Those gathered around Jesus see his words as gracious, thinking that he is proclaiming good news for them alone (verse 22). Soon, though, Jesus angers the crowd by including examples of Gentiles who have found a place in the work of God:

> But the truth is, there were many widows in Israel in the time of Elijah, when the heaven was shut up three years and six months, and there was a severe famine over all the land; yet Elijah was sent to none of them except to a widow at Zarephath in Sidon. There were also many lepers in Israel in the time of the prophet Elisha, and none of them was cleansed except Naaman the Syrian.   (Luke 4.25–27).

In both the examples Jesus gives, the Gentiles were dealt with more graciously by God than by the Israelites, and it is made plain that God uses non-Jews in God's own mission.

This is not acceptable to those in the synagogue, who see themselves as victims who have God on their side. The Jews feel particularly victimized by the Romans, so they want a Messiah who will help (only) them. Yet as victims, they themselves are victimizing others within their own communities and outside, due to their narrow attitudes and the boundaries they have put in place.

Learning to see God on the other side

One essential fact that challenges the idea that God is only on our side is that we are all made in the image of God. If we genuinely believe this, we cannot think that God is on our side against another human being who has also been created in God's image.

However, we frequently assume that God is on our side in day-to-day life. We want to see God fighting our battles against other people. Even in church, something I come across frequently is people saying that someone who dared oppose them has had trouble visited upon them by God. They believe that this has happened because God is with the one opposed. Such an understanding of God is certainly very narrow.

It is good to believe that God is on our side, but it is dangerous and unbiblical to believe that God is *only* on our side (ruling out the possibility that God can be with others), and that God is always on our side *against* others. Both views are problematic. God with us is not God with us against all others. God can be with us, and God can be with others – whom we may not like, or whom we think may not like us.

In fact we should want God to be with us – there is nothing wrong with that. A yearning that God is with us affirms and strengthens our faith. The problem arises when we think that God is only on our side and we want God to be on our side against the other – that leads to us building boundaries and limiting God within us.

Whenever someone thinks God is on their side, God is on the other side too. The concept of who is in and who is out comes easily to us, but whenever we find ourselves thinking in such a way, let us remember that God is on the 'out' side too. It is difficult to accept this, but we could try to put ourselves on the other side and consider how it feels. Someone once said, 'every time you draw a line between who's in and who's out, you'll find Jesus on the other side.'

We may feel we are in trouble if we see God on the other side, although this is a crucial requirement for the ministry of reconciliation. Overcoming the division of us and them – or self and other – is a huge challenge. When we perceive that God already transcends the boundaries *we* have (perhaps unwittingly) constructed, our work of reconciliation will move forward greatly.

Questions for reflection

1 Have you ever prayed for people you don't like and think do not like you? How do you feel when you do that? How do you understand God during such times?
2 In what ways can 'God is on the other side' helpfully impact on our faith in 'God on our side'?
3 How do we respond when we come across incidents where some (or we) may believe God is on our side against someone?

7

Reconciliation as peace with justice

Reconciliation, whether interpersonal or intercommunity, is directly connected to our own well-being – the peace we feel within. Thus in the context of intergroup conflict, we are prompted to work for reconciliation because conflict ultimately affects us all, whether or not we are participating in it. Conflict is a problem for the whole world, and it is a problem for us. Similarly, in the context of interpersonal conflict, we desire reconciliation when we feel distressed or guilty, or when we realize that we are willing to humble ourselves to seek forgiveness from those with whom we are in conflict. We want to be at peace with the other so we can be at peace with ourselves. However, one of the main difficulties we face in resolving conflicts is that, at some point, reconciliation has to be balanced with justice. The problem is that everyone wants peace (for themselves), but most want it without justice (for others). Yet reconciliation and justice can never be separated. The Psalmist affirms that 'righteousness and peace will kiss each other' (Ps 85.10) to express that peace is not possible without justice.

To affirm the importance of peace with justice for the Christian ministry of reconciliation, we need to appreciate three things: the dangers of a simplistic view of peace, the distinction between reconciliation and forgiveness, and the fact that reconciliation is vertical (with God) and horizontal (with our fellow human beings) at the same time.

First, peace is not the absence of conflict and violence, and reconciliation does not involve denying the legitimacy of having differences and disagreements. Peace and reconciliation lose their power if they relate only to an absence of tension and violence. A simple peace, involving no conflict, can exist merely because those who are dominant have rendered the weak voiceless. Yet this is not peace. The biblical understanding of shalom is holistic and dynamic: it not the absence of violence, but rather life in its fullness – with equality and justice for all. It is living and flourishing in community. Disagreements and differences are possible, but because justice is maintained there is peace. Genuine reconciliation relates to being at peace with others, even when they are different from us and when we may not agree with everything they say.

Some think that reconciliation involves not revisiting past conflicts and not reopening old wounds, and that such avoidance will promote the process of healing; but there is a problem with this. A circumstance may occur when an old wound will simply burst out! The Truth and Reconciliation Commission in South Africa (there are similar initiatives in different parts of the world) may have had limitations, but it demonstrated how to bring together reconciliation and justice for those who had been victimized. 'Truth' stood for justice and there was an attempt to expose the damage done to the vulnerable during conflicts, even while genuine efforts towards reconciliation were made.

Second, reconciliation in the context of interpersonal conflict and broken relationships is not about simply seeking forgiveness from the victim. It is certainly important to recognize and admit one's mistakes, but reconciliation is complete only when the victim is able to forgive. What often stands between seeking forgiveness and reconciliation relates to the question of justice. Forgiveness cannot bypass justice. When we are the offender, we are obliged to act justly and to seek to make amends, while asking for forgiveness.

However, when we are in a position to forgive, not to forgive is injustice. Human beings created by God often go astray and this affects the communities in which we live. We are constantly in the process of seeking forgiveness from God and from others, and hopefully in the process of forgiving others in turn. (If we think we do not need forgiveness, then we may be quite a long way from God and quite detached from our community.) While we need to be open to forgiving others, we cannot compel those we have offended to forgive us. One cannot demand forgiveness.

Third, reconciliation is both vertical and horizontal at the same time. We can never be at peace with God if we are not at peace with our neighbours, and being at peace with our neighbours means, by default, behaving justly towards them. This plain and simple message runs through the Bible, but it is not easy for us to follow. Often, when we seek the joy of communion with God, we manage to ignore the fact that we have hardened our hearts towards our fellow human beings. Reconciling with God seems easy, while reconciling with those with whom we are in conflict presents huge difficulties. We are concerned to seek God's forgiveness for our sins without regarding the impact those sins have had on others.

This chapter begins with the message of the prophets in Israel and Judah, who unambiguously declared that peace with God involves acting justly towards our fellow human beings. These things are two sides of the same coin. God is not interested in people reconciling with God through appealing to the many covenants God has made with the forefathers and mothers of the Israelites, or through ritual, worship, fasting and sacrifices. Jesus' encounter with the Syrophoenician woman illustrates that his concern is peace with justice, and only when the woman is able to accept this does the healing of her daughter become possible. David's dealings with Absalom and his other children show what happens when reconciliation comes about without justice being displayed to the victims.

The story of Zacchaeus is a wonderful example of reconciliation with God and our fellow human beings on the one hand, and restorative justice on the other. Jacob is in a position to seek reconciliation with his brother Esau for cheating him out of his blessings twice, and Jacob's journey back home vividly depicts the fear and difficulty he experiences until justice is done. The generosity Esau shows in forgiving and accepting Jacob plays a large part in their reconciliation. While forgiveness is not a substitute for justice, when we are in a position to forgive others, it is unjust not to do so.

Finally, although seeking forgiveness from God is an essential part of our personal and collective life, justice demands that we also recognize and repent of the damage our sins have done to others.

34 Peace with God, justice to fellow humans

Key texts:
- Isaiah 1.11–17; 58.1–14
- Micah 6.6–8
- Amos 5.18–27

The theme of peace with justice is expressed nowhere better in the Bible than in the message of the prophets, particularly those who lived around the eighth century BC. The Israelites – or at least the dominant, privileged elite – believed that their covenantal relationship with God, their status of being the chosen people, and the strength of their worship, rituals, sacrifices, offerings, fasting, prayers and songs meant they were at peace with God, and that this would ensure them much blessing. Yet the prophets of God have to convey to these Israelites the difficult message that God is not interested in peace on such terms. Rather, God condemns their ritual practices and prayers if these are not accompanied by justice to their fellow Israelites and others, especially the poor and needy among them.

The Israelite elite thought that their relationship with God was secure and that God's everlasting blessings would never cease. This was primarily because of the covenantal relationship God had made with their forefathers and mothers, which promised blessings for their descendants for generations. What they failed to realize was that these covenants were never simply between God and an individual; rather, individuals were seen as part of a collective community, either in the present or in the future. The covenants of God were always to remind the Israelites to live in good relationship with God and with others, but while they wanted to claim blessings from God, privileged Israelites did not want to care for the poor and the vulnerable. They thought they could make peace with God by going to the temple, worshipping God, offering sacrifices and singing praises and songs – and they went on adding to the number of the festivals they celebrated.

One of the main tasks of the prophets was to help people understand that making peace with God goes alongside practising justice towards others. The two are completely interconnected. The eighth century prophets in Judah and Israel repeatedly maintained that seeking peace with God in the manner of the Israelite elite was no good if they were not acting justly towards their fellow human beings. Their rituals were an abomination to God in such circumstances – they were useless without righteous acts before God.

We have seen that the Israelite community was built on covenant with God, but a covenantal relationship has to be both vertical and horizontal at the same time. God's love endures but people are accountable to God and there is an expectation that they will live in communion with their fellow human beings. Many of the Israelites had abandoned – or at least lost sight of – their accountability and covenantal responsibility, and a covenant does not save when justice is not done.

Most of the judgements of God pronounced by the prophets concerned the injustice meted out to the poor, the disadvantaged and the needy. There was particular condemnation of the attitudes of the rich and powerful, as these served only to increase the deprivation of those at the bottom of the social ladder. Prophets like Amos, Isaiah, Micah, Jeremiah and Hosea repeatedly talk about the judgements of God towards those involved in oppressing others: they trampled the poor, took bribes (Amos 5.11, 8.4), oppressed the poor (Micah 3.3, 9–10), robbed them (Isaiah 3.14) and grabbed land from others to extend their own lands (Isaiah 5.8).

The prophet Micah says that burnt offerings, or offerings of calves, or rams or oil – all precious and expensive – will not please God in the slightest. Nor even will the offering of a first born child. In one of the most memorable prophetic pronouncements, Micah says that it is justice, mercy and humility that God requires.

> With what shall I come before the LORD, and bow myself before God on high?
> Shall I come before him with burnt offerings, with calves a year old?
> Will the LORD be pleased with thousands of rams, with ten thousands of rivers of oil?
> Shall I give my firstborn for my transgression, the fruit of my body for the sin of my soul?'
> He has told you, O mortal, what is good; and what does the LORD require of you but to do justice, and to love kindness, and to walk humbly with your God? (Micah 6.6–8)

Perhaps it is Amos who most strongly links peace with God and justice to our fellow human beings. He says that God is not interested in the festivals, assemblies, Sabbath songs, music and praises of the

Israelites, or with their offerings of grain and fatted animals. Rather, God's concern is with letting justice for the poor 'roll down like waters':

> I hate, I despise your festivals, and I take no delight in your solemn assemblies.
> Even though you offer me your burnt offerings and grain offerings, I will not accept them;
> and the offerings of well-being of your fatted animals I will not look upon.
> Take away from me the noise of your songs; I will not listen to the melody of your harps.
> But let justice roll down like waters, and righteousness like an ever-flowing stream. (Amos 5.21–24).

Similarly, the prophet Isaiah challenges the Israelite elite about their disregard of justice. God hates their multitude of sacrifices, festivals and assemblies, Sabbath and prayers. He says, what is acceptable to God is seeking justice, rescuing the oppressed, defending the orphan and pleading for the widows:

> What to me is the multitude of your sacrifices? says the LORD;
> I have had enough of burnt offerings of rams and the fat of fed beasts;
> I do not delight in the blood of bulls, or of lambs, or of goats.
> When you come to appear before me, who asked this from your hand?
> Trample my courts no more; bringing offerings is futile;
> incense is an abomination to me.
> New moon and sabbath and calling of convocation –
> I cannot endure solemn assemblies with iniquity.
> Your new moons and your appointed festivals my soul hates;
> they have become a burden to me, I am weary of bearing them.
> When you stretch out your hands, I will hide my eyes from you;
> even though you make many prayers, I will not listen;
> your hands are full of blood.
> Wash yourselves; make yourselves clean;
> remove the evil of your doings from before my eyes;
> cease to do evil, learn to do good;
> seek justice, rescue the oppressed,
> defend the orphan, plead for the widow. (Isaiah 1.11–17).

In another context, Isaiah makes a full-length attack on the ritual of fasting, clarifying that fasting does not please God:

Is not this the fast that I choose: to loose the bonds of injustice,
to undo the thongs of the yoke, to let the oppressed go free,
and to break every yoke?
Is it not to share your bread with the hungry,
and bring the homeless poor into your house;
when you see the naked, to cover them,
and not to hide yourself from your own kin?   (Isaiah 58.6–7)

If you offer your food to the hungry
and satisfy the needs of the afflicted,
then your light shall rise in the darkness
and your gloom be like the noonday.   (Isaiah 58.10)

Jeremiah and Hosea join the other prophets in condemning the privileged Israelites' current practices. Jeremiah pronounces God's words that 'Although they fast, I do not hear their cry, and although they offer burnt offering and grain offering, I do not accept them' (Jeremiah 14.12). In fact, not only are they failing to care for the poor, these Israelites are unfairly profiting from the sale of offerings and sacrifices to those who can least afford them. The prophet Hosea warns that sacrifices do not help to secure God's blessings. God is not willing to accept them when the Israelites have gone astray (Hosea 8.13).

The prophets' attacks on ritual should not be taken to mean that God is displeased with ritual and worship. The problem is simply that some people are worshipping God and offering sacrifices while behaving unjustly to others, and as God hates injustice, such actions cannot be approved. It is important to remember what Jesus said later in a similar context – that offerings (or more broadly speaking, rituals) are acceptable if one is not neglecting to practise justice:

Woe to you, scribes and Pharisees, hypocrites! For you tithe mint, dill, and cummin, and have neglected the weightier matters of the law: justice and mercy and faith. It is these you ought to have practised without neglecting the others. You blind guides! You strain out a gnat but swallow a camel!   (Matthew 23.23–24)

The Prophets of the Old Testament clearly show that peace with God equates to justice to our fellow human beings and to creation. Yet quite often, Christians have not seen the way in which we commonly disconnect peace and justice as a problem.

For centuries, many Christians in the West failed to understand that slavery and injustice to others was incompatible with peace with God. The image of Bible-reading Christian slave owners telling their slaves how to behave and be obedient, and then praying to God for them, is a really troubling image. Similarly, in the Indian context, I have wondered why followers of the influential Advaitic concept of the oneness of Brahamn, the Supreme Being, which is concerned with unity behind diversity in all that exists in the universe, were not prompted to challenge the discrimination based on caste and gender they could see around them.

The truth is that we have participated in slavery, colonialism, empire-building, violence and war, along with everyday discrimination based on gender, race, ethnicity and religion. It may be difficult for us to accept this, and we may feel the need to put such matters out of our mind, or to come up with excuses; either way, we are not balancing peace with God and justice to our neighbour.

The people of God in the Old Testament thought they were at peace with God, but they were not, until they acted justly towards one another. The prophetic message is clear: if you want peace, you need to act justly. Justice is an inevitable part of peace, and peace with God and peace within are dependent on being at peace with others.

Questions for reflection

1 How is the message of the prophets, that peace with God involves behaving justly to our fellow human beings, relevant today?

2 Why are we tempted not to mind the common disconnection of these two?

3 Jesus says that 'you ought to have practised without neglecting the others.' Reflect on the importance of connecting worship and justice in your Christian life.

35 Peace expects justice

Key text: Mark 7.24–30
Jesus and the Syrophoenician woman

This miracle story is about Jesus crossing boundaries to enter a hostile place – the regions of Tyre and Sidon. These Gentile cities, north of Israel in Phoenicia, are not in a good relationship with Galilee, but Jesus takes the initiative in an attempt to improve communications and bring about reconciliation. However, his subsequent conversation with the Syrophoenician woman, who comes to Jesus (although actually he has come to her) asking for healing for her daughter, is quite odd compared to other healing stories. Their conversation about bread, read in the light of the socio-economic background of the region, encompasses not only healing, but also justice. Thus, one insight we gain is that Jesus' interest in peace breaking out between the conflicting territories is connected to a desire for justice to be done in order for peace to happen.

Generally, this passage is regarded as marking Jesus' move into mission to the Gentiles, although he has already healed the Centurion's servant (Matthew 8.5–13; Luke 7.1–10) and linked the Nazareth Manifesto to the Gentiles (Luke 4.16–30).

The encounter with the Syrophoenician woman is regarded as rather a disturbing incident in the Bible for many of us. Jesus' words that 'it is not fair to take the children's food and throw it to the dogs' seem harsh: not only is he refusing to heal, in the first instance at least, he also seems to be using the word dog to refer to the child who is in need. At no other time is Jesus seen to deny help (and in such a manner – he could simply have said no!) Jesus has always crossed boundaries and reached out to sinners, lepers, tax collectors, women caught in adultery and others. There is no record of him using such strong, demeaning words to refer to them. Here again, it is Jesus who has crossed boundaries to go to a hostile region. How then could he speak in this manner to a woman who is asking him for help for her ailing child?

To understand what is happening between Jesus and the Syrophoenician woman, it is important to focus on the difficult words, rather than read the story simply as relating to a miracle or a mission to the Gentiles. The woman asks for healing, but Jesus talks about children (note he is referring to a group of people) and contrasts what he is saying with what the woman is asking for. It is ironic that in refusing to heal a child, he refers to the welfare of children. The woman asks for a demon to be chased out of her daughter so that she may be healed, yet Jesus talks about bread. The connection is quite surprising: demon and bread! Then very shockingly, Jesus uses the reference to dogs, seemingly to despise the woman to her face. Jesus does employ harsh words in other contexts, only against those who refused to listen to him or trust him (the elite groups) or understand him (his disciples) – never towards a woman pleading for help for her little daughter.

Jesus' use of terms such as bread, feeding, crumbs and dog require us to look more closely at the socio-economic background of first century Palestine.

First, there were often tensions between the Jews and the Tyrians. In the writings of Josephus, we find that the Tyrians were the bitterest enemies of the Jews. Many Jews were killed and imprisoned in the Roman-Jewish wars, which further increased enmity. There was also a belief in ancient Israel and in post-exilic Judaism that the Phoenician and Canaanite merchants (including those from Tyre) who imported luxury, alien cults and ritual impurities into the country would never be allowed to enter the house of Yahweh.

Second, the economic relationship between the poor Jewish peasants in Galilee and the wealthy Tyrians should also be considered. The Old Testament, backed by archaeological evidence, bears witness to Tyre being a rich city that traded extensively with the whole Mediterranean region. However, as it was on the coast the possibilities for farming were very limited, and for agricultural produce, Tyre had to depend upon other countries. In the Old Testament we see that Solomon sends wheat and oil to Hiram of Tyre (1 Kings 5.11). Ezekiel also confirms the export of food products to Tyre from Judah and Israel (Ezekiel 27.17). In Acts 12.20, we see the Tyrians depending on Herod for their food. Archaeological findings and rabbinic sources also confirm the export of grain from Galilee to Tyre. At the time of the Roman-Jewish wars, supplying the Hellenistic coastal cities left the poor Jewish peasants of Galilee in want of food.

Thus, the conversation between Jesus and the Syrophoenician woman about bread highlights economic exploitation. Jesus' words, 'let the children be fed first, for it is not fair to take the children's food and throw it to the dogs' imply he believes the poor Jewish peasants, who are the real owners of the food, should be fed, and that it is not good to supply this to the rich Tyrians. He is reminding the woman of the exploitation carried out by her own people. For Jews, a dog is an unclean animal that roams around the streets and scavenges for food. Such is the injustice done to the poor people of Galilee that Jesus goes to the extent of harshly calling their exploiters 'dogs'.

The woman comes to Jesus seeking his help, but it is important to consider her social status. Generally, she is seen as a poor and helpless woman whose request for help was rejected (at least initially). However, many biblical scholars consider she may have come from a quite wealthy background. It is interesting to see Mark identifying her as Greek (Hellene), that is, someone who was of above average status in first century Palestine. Moreover, the word used for the bed of the woman's daughter is a grandiose *kli/nh* (couch), and not a *kra/batton* (mattress), which we come across in other stories of healing (Mark 2.4, 9, 12; 6.55). This means that the Syrophoenician woman was a member of the privileged, educated upper class, unlike most of the other women who came to Jesus for help.

Finally, what exactly does the woman say? How does she effect a change of heart in Jesus? Her words, 'even the dogs under the table eat the children's crumbs', indicate that she accepts the bread belongs to the children. She understands that the poor Jewish peasants are the real owners of the food, and they need to be fed first before the surplus may be exported to the Tyrians. Although Jesus uses the word 'dogs' in accordance with his cultural understanding, the woman's background means she understands 'dogs' as 'pet animals', which are humbly waiting under the table for crumbs from their master. She accepts that the Tyrians are dependent on the poor Jewish peasants for their food. Her words are an affirmation of justice, and this is what Jesus requires to heal her daughter and thus extend his work of peacemaking in the region.

What this story tells us is that the injustice meted out to poor Galilean peasants by rich Tyrians is an important concern for Jesus, even while he is interested in peace between the regions. Jesus does not want the rich to live at the expense of the poor: his mission for peace is wholly underpinned by the expectation of justice.

Questions for reflection

1   Do you get the impression from this story that Jesus is reluctant to heal Gentiles?

2   How do we understand conversion in a wider sense? Consider how the woman and Jesus interact and how their perceptions seem to change in the process.

3   The woman's response: humility, openness and accepting justice. Reflect on the importance of these for genuine reconciliation.

36 When justice is not done

Key texts: 2 Samuel 13–14
David and his children

If you want an example of an utter disregard for justice, compounded by a rush for superficial reconciliation, leading to events spiralling out of control, look no further than the affairs of David, Absalom and David's other children recorded in 2 Samuel 13 and 14. Here it becomes apparent that David is disinterested in justice, contenting himself with a shallow reconciliation without addressing the concerns of justice for those who have been wronged.

The story is this. After David seeks God's forgiveness for his sin against Bathsheba and Uriah, several things happen that affect his children's relationships with one another and with their father. David's son Amnon rapes his half sister Tamar, sister of Absalom, another son of David. David does nothing in response, and after some time, Absalom takes revenge on Amnon by killing him. He then flees, but Joab, the commander of David's army, knowing that David yearns for Absalom, arranges to reconcile the two. David agrees to the reconciliation, but doesn't allow Absalom to come into his presence and see his face. Absalom is irritated by this, although he does eventually get a chance to enter the presence of the king. Later Absalom attempts to grab power and forces David to flee Jerusalem. The story ends when the same Joab who mediated reconciliation between David and Absalom kills Absalom to save David!

Power struggles are not uncommon in ancient (and modern) kingdoms, and they certainly occurred in David's family. However, his family's affairs show that when justice is repeatedly denied, although reconciliation is attempted, disaster is sure to follow.

The first injustice is done when David does not take action over what has happened to his daughter, Tamar. Of course, he gets angry when he hears of it, but as her father, he seems strangely unconcerned for her welfare. The status of women in ancient Jewish society was generally low, and the attitude towards rape tended to be either silence or indifference. Yet Tamar's words to Amnon reveal that rape was actually a crime. She tells him, 'No, my brother, do not force me; for such a thing is not done in Israel; do not do anything so vile!' (2 Samuel 13.12). Neither the gravity of Amnon's assault nor the rarity of this kind of attack in Israel make David remonstrate appropriately on behalf of his daughter.

David is not willing to confront Amnon, let alone punish him for what he did. Verse 21 says that, 'When King David heard of all these things, he became very angry, *but he would not punish his son Amnon, because he loved him, for he was his firstborn.*' His love for Amnon consigns Tamar to the sidelines. In the previous chapter of 2 Samuel, God showed David clearly that his sins against Bathsheba and her husband Uriah were not right in the sight of God. Yet in spite of this, David does not dare to seek justice for his daughter.

Before the assault took place, David took time to visit Amnon when he was pretending to be ill (and requested, disastrously, that Tamar should to go and cook for him). However, after the event, we do not see David visiting Tamar to offer her comfort, let alone assure her of justice. It does not seem to matter to him that Tamar remains 'a desolate woman' in her brother Absalom's house (verse 20), or that she has removed her royal robe and is not coming into the royal place. He simply does not want to confront or punish Amnon.

Second, David fails to perceive the enmity Absalom feels towards Amnon for raping his sister. When Absalom asks David to send Amnon (with all the king's other sons) to the feast at the sheep shearing, David fails to consider whether Absalom is actually at peace with Amnon. It does not seem to strike him that justice has never been done to Tamar and that Absalom remains angry with Amnon.

Third, when Amnon is killed, David is worried that all his sons have died. Relief comes when he knows that only Amnon is dead. Absalom flees, and after some years have passed, David starts to yearn for him. We read, 'And the heart of the king went out, yearning for Absalom; for he was now consoled over the death of Amnon' (2 Samuel 13.39). It is only a matter of time before David switches his love and affection to another, but *the matter of justice* remains unaddressed.

Finally, when Joab learns that David's heart yearns for Absalom, he performs a trick to make David bring Absalom back – and another act of false reconciliation happens! David agrees to Absalom's return, but he does not want to talk to him. He tells Joab, 'Let him go to his own house, he is not to come into my presence'. Perhaps David intends this to be a punishment for what Absalom did? Not allowing Absalom to see the king's face may be denying him a mark of blessing and assurance of forgiveness. However, it also robs David of an opportunity to confront Absalom about what he did, just as he earlier failed to confront Amnon. David seems to lack the will and courage to tell his sons that what they did was not right. Twice he fails to perform acts of justice for the victims in this story. As a result, Absalom goes to his own house, and because he is irritated about Joab not coming as requested to send him to the king, he burns Joab's field in anger. When Joab meets Absalom, Absalom tells him 'now let me go into the king's presence. If there is guilt in me, let him kill me' (14.32). Even then, David is unable to tell Absalom that what he did to Amnon was wrong; instead 'the king kissed Absalom' (verse 33).

Perhaps this story is really about a king forgiving his *sons* for what they did. David may have some justification in the context of whom he wants to succeed him. Thus, he forgives Amnon for what he did to Tamar, and Absalom for what he did to Amnon. Offering forgiveness without showing justice to the victims, though, along with seeking to reconcile without demonstrating courage (even on the part of a king) to confront the offenders, actually lead to a spiral of events that result in a greater crisis in David's life and kingdom. This example of false reconciliation shows what happens when justice is denied while offenders are heartily embraced.

Questions for reflection

1   What do you think David should have done for Tamar?
2   When Absalom returns, David does not allow him to see his face. In what ways do you think this might disconcert Absalom?
3   What we can do to avoid becoming involved in shallow reconciliation that does not offer justice to those who have been offended?

37 Restoration and reconciliation

Key text: Luke 19.1–10
Jesus and Zacchaeus

Reconciliation involves more than expressing remorse and seeking forgiveness – it needs an act of restoration towards those victimized to be complete. The story of Zacchaeus is a wonderful example of reconciliation with restoration. This tax collector, who eagerly seeks salvation from Christ, demonstrates his understanding of two crucial aspects of reconciliation. First, he shows that reconciling with God and seeking God's salvation is strongly related to reconciling with our fellow human beings. Second, he very actively takes part in committing himself to restoring what he has taken from his victims, thus bringing justice to the centre of the reconciliation process. Allan Aubrey Boesak calls what Zacchaeus displays 'radical reconciliation'.

Zacchaeus was a Jew, working for the Romans. In the first century, tax was a great burden for the common people, both because of the economic pressure of paying various taxes, and because of the unscrupulous ways in which those involved in collecting taxes creamed off money for themselves. Being close to the Roman authorities, the tax collectors were unconcerned about the distress their cheating and exploitation caused. However, although rich, they were reviled. Common people naturally did not want to relate with them, the poor hated them for plundering their meagre resources, and the Jewish elites regarded them as impure and unclean because they mingled with the Romans.

A realization that leads to reconciliation

Zacchaeus would have been despised by his fellow Jews and it is very interesting that he takes the initiative to come and see Jesus. Perhaps he realizes that he doesn't have much peace and regrets that people think poorly of him in spite of his wealth. Surely if money had meant everything to him, he would not have sought out Jesus. Zacchaeus may have been curious to know what kind of man Jesus was because Jesus accepted sinners and mingled with them; he entered their homes and ate with them. Zacchaeus may be experiencing an awakening self-awareness and a longing for acceptance and friendship. There has to be a strong reason for him to make the effort he does. He cannot mingle with the crowd because he is too short to see; furthermore, the people would not accept him and he may, in fact, have been at some physical risk, such is the bad feeling he has aroused.

Jesus finds Zacchaeus, even though he is up a sycamore tree. When Jesus tells him to come down because he wants to stay at his house, Zacchaeus immediately obeys and goes with Jesus. The crowd grumbles that the Lord has gone to the place of a sinner like Zacchaeus, but Zacchaeus does not complain (verse 7). He understands perfectly well why the people grumble. He might think they have every right to do so considering how he has exploited them. He genuinely appreciates the difficulty involved in people accepting him. It is significant that when he begins talking, he does not respond to the crowd by defending himself. In fact, he is unable to face them. Neither does Jesus prompt him in any way. Jesus just silently observes what the crowd is saying and listens when Zacchaeus tells him what he intends to do for the people. Words are no use, only action will suffice. Zacchaeus knows this. He is coming to terms with his role in creating a situation of conflict and this realization leads him to come to Jesus and to initiate the next steps for reconciliation.

Restoration and reconciliation

Zacchaeus stands as an example of one who is willing to make restoration and reimbursement part of the reconciliation process. He tells Jesus that if he has defrauded anyone of anything, he is prepared to pay back four times as much. He has already promised to pay half his wealth to the poor. He wants reconciliation with Jesus and with his victims that is based around an act of restitution. He does not think twice about what it will cost him. If reconciliation is to take place, especially in the context of socio-economic injustice as happens here, a real payback to the victims is important in order to restore justice.

Today, in the context of conflicts involving economic exploitation and inequality, restoration is the tricky thing that often halts the process of a proper reconciliation. Those who are in positions of privilege – generally through exploiting others – can find it difficult to sacrifice their privilege to make restitution to the victims. Zacchaeus' story shows the importance of restoration as an act of justice in the process of reconciliation. Of course Zacchaeus' act of restoration is not his generosity, but his generosity is essential for reconciliation because it is appropriate and just.

Wealth is not a stumbling block for reconciliation

Zacchaeus' reconciliation with God and with his victims assures us that wealth is not a stumbling block for reconciliation. Generally, wealth is one significant factor that contributes to conflict (as with Zacchaeus defrauding others to increase his own wealth), and it often stands in the way of reconciliation. In some of the other passages we have reflected upon in this book, wealth contributes to conflict. Greed for wealth, as in the Abraham-Lot story, keeps reconciliation and proper relationships at bay. Yet Zacchaeus shows us that wealth does not need to affect the process of reconciliation. He reminds us that if wealth stands as the reason for conflict, it can also facilitate reconciliation. He is rich (verse 2), but agrees to give half of his wealth to the poor. He is willing to pay people four times what he has cheated them out of. What he intends to pay to bring about restoration is an enormous part of what he has. Contrast this with another rich man in the Bible. Only in the previous chapter of Luke, we read of a rich man who is unable to follow Jesus because he is unwilling to spend his wealth on the poor (Luke 18.18–25).

Reconciliation and salvation

Salvation is possible when reconciliation takes place. When Zacchaeus says that he is willing to restore what he has taken from the people, Jesus says: 'Today salvation has come to this house, because he too is a son of Abraham' (verse 9). This title is an honour for Zacchaeus, especially as he has been rejected by his fellow Jews as impure and is not welcome among them. Jesus reinstates him as an acceptable person among those in his community, but only when Zacchaeus repents of what he has been doing to his victims, initiates restoration and is willing to share his wealth to bring this about.

In some western countries, the abolition of slavery and the freeing of slaves was an important development in the nineteenth century, bringing relief to hundreds of thousands who were exploited for generations. However, the sad part is that they were never restored properly. Freeing them has not been enough. They were left with nothing when slavery was abolished, and they and their descendants were never compensated for what had been done to them. Slave owners, however, were compensated for losing their 'property' in a way that increased their huge wealth. Justice is yet to be done fully for the victims of slavery. Slavery should never have happened in the first place, obviously, but its abolition was a great achievement. However, reconciliation between the descendents of the victims and the descendants of the slave owners has yet to come about. There are similar circumstances all over the world where injustice stands in the way of reconciliation between offenders and victims. Reconciliation is possible only with just and proper restoration for the latter.

'Whatever happened has happened; let us now move forward' is a statement we often come across in the context of reconciliation after conflict. Such moving forward is good for the offender or the privileged, but not for any victims carrying wounds and the memory of loss. Many reconciliation processes do not last long because restoration is lacking. Zacchaeus' radical reconciliation remains a great model to follow in such contexts.

Questions for reflection

1 Are you conscious of making excuses when you know that you have deprived someone of something, benefitted out of that and need to restore it, if you want to receive forgiveness from your victim and from God?
2 In what ways can our wealth help enrich our ministry of reconciliation?
3 Why is our salvation inherently connected with our ministry of reconciliation and restoration?

38 Fear, magnanimity and justice

Key text: Genesis 32–33
Jacob reconciling with Esau

The story of reconciliation between the brothers Esau and Jacob has several important lessons for us. Jacob's journey of returning home involves recognizing the injustice he committed against Esau when he cheated him out of his birthright and their father's blessings. Whether Jacob wants this injustice corrected or not, his travels are undoubtedly marked by agonizing anxiety. Jacob is uncertain as to how Esau will react when they are face to face, and in some ways, Jacob's fear continues even after his meeting with Esau ends much better than expected. However, the story also records the often underplayed generosity of Esau in accepting Jacob, in spite of the fact that Jacob has cheated him twice. In fact, it is Esau's magnanimity that turns Jacob's fearful journey into one of reconciliation. In short, we witness how an offender feels in the process of reconciliation, and see a victim making reconciliation complete through offering forgiveness and acceptance.

Jacob knows that acceptance by his brother is essential if he is to return home, but he is troubled as to how this is going to come about. He knows that the injustice he has done is still not rectified, and his fear is evident in the many actions he takes as he cautiously draws closer to Esau.

First, the way in which Jacob instructs the servants he dispatches to meet with Esau shows how fearful he is. He sends them ahead so they may seek Esau's favour by giving him a brief account of Jacob's stay with Laban. Laban does not come out of this well: Jacob says he lived with him as an alien (32.4). Perhaps he is seeking to arouse pity in Esau and reassure him that he has never forgotten his home, although he has been away for many years. Later, when Jacob learns that Esau is coming to meet him, he again sends servants ahead of him, this time bearing gifts. He tells each of them not to forget to say that 'Moreover your servant Jacob is behind us' (verses 18, 20). He takes pains to give these very carefully worded instructions.

Second, when Jacob hears that Esau is coming with 400 men, he is greatly distressed (32.7). He assumes Esau proposes to attack him, his wives and his children and to ransack his belongings. Jacob immediately arranges for his people and possessions to be divided into two camps so that, even if Esau attacks one, the other will escape (verse 8). Such is the state of Jacob's conscience that he can only think Esau comes to destroy him, though Esau actually approaches his brother with a kind and welcoming heart.

Third, Jacob prays to God to deliver him from the hands of his brother (verses 9–12) without even knowing why Esau is coming. It is interesting to see that God does not appear to Esau to warn him that he should not harm Jacob, in the way he appeared earlier to warn Laban (Genesis 31.24). Rather, it seems God wants Jacob to go through this journey of realization.

Fourth, out of fear, Jacob tries to appease Esau with many gifts (32.13–15). Unlike Zacchaeus, Jacob does not openly acknowledge that he has cheated his victim, but he does send a lot to try to make up for stealing the rights and blessings that were due to Esau.

Fifth, Jacob repeatedly uses the term 'your servant' to refer to himself (32.4, 18; 33.5), and 'lord' to refer to Esau (32.4, 18; 33.8). When he comes before Esau, he bows down continuously seven times (33.3), which seems quite formal and excessive. Jacob then flatters Esau, saying 'to see your face is like seeing the face of God' (33.10). Rarely do we come across one brother addressing and respecting the other in such a way.

Finally, Jacob's fear seems to continue even after he has been magnanimously accepted by his brother. He is keen that Esau departs and sets off ahead of him. When Esau proposes to leave some of his people to be of assistance to Jacob, Jacob declines the offer. He wants Esau and his people away and, contrary to his promise to Esau that he would come slowly and meet him in Seir, he changes direction, goes to Succoth and settles there (33.17).

The story of Esau and Jacob shows that Jacob is aware of the mistakes he has made. On the positive side, his fear expresses a realization that he has cheated his brother and needs to put this right before he meets him again. On several occasions he thinks and speaks of gaining favour from Esau. Sadly, however, Jacob never throws off his fear, even after Esau accepts him and is willing to help him.

Esau is the hero of this reconciliation story. He comes to meet Jacob when he knows Jacob is returning home, and while Jacob bows down seven times when they see each other, Esau runs to meet his brother (33.4), embraces him, falls on his neck and kisses him. It is plain he has been missing Jacob, in spite of the fact that Jacob cheated him. Esau wonders why his brother feels the need to meet him with gifts. 'What do you mean by all this company I met?' (verse 8). The message is that there's no need for Jacob to go to such extravagant lengths to reconcile with Esau. As he expresses it most beautifully, 'I have enough, my brother, keep what you have for yourself' (verse 9). In spite of Jacob stealing his birthright and the blessings from his father, Esau says he has plenty. Of course, Esau is still rich, but these words are generous and magnanimous indeed. The final confirmation and affirmation of reconciliation actually comes from Esau: 'Let *us* journey on *our way*, I will go *alongside* you' (verse 12). Jacob turns down this suggestion, however, as well as Esau's offer to leave some of his people to be helpful (verse 15). It is the character of Esau that stands out when it comes to forgiveness and reconciliation between these two brothers.

Esau accepts Jacob without minding what Jacob has done to him. Even though Jacob's realization of his injustice to Esau – and his journey to meet him – make this one of the greatest reconciliation stories, Esau's attitude of accepting and forgiving Jacob is in striking contrast to the way in which Jacob continues to live in a state of some fear.

Questions for reflection

1 Why do you think God did not warn Esau in the way he warned Laban earlier?
2 Is Jacob's enduring fear justifiable? Why is he unable to overcome this in spite of Esau's forgiveness? How do we cope with fear when reconciliation proves very difficult?
3 What does Esau's magnanimity teach us about reconciliation?

39 To forgive is to do justice

Key text: Matthew 18.23–35
The unforgiving servant who was forgiven

Forgiveness by itself is not reconciliation, and an offender seeking forgiveness from a victim alone is not justice in the context of reconciliation. As we have reflected in previous studies, forgiveness without justice results in a cheap and shallow reconciliation. However, not to forgive is injustice: if we want to receive forgiveness from someone, but are not willing to forgive a person who needs forgiveness from us, then we act unfairly. This is what the parable in Matthew 18.23–35 teaches us, through the story of a servant who seeks and receives forgiveness from his lord, but is not willing to forgive someone who is in a much worse condition than he is.

Peter asks Jesus, 'Lord, if another member of the church sins against me, how often should I forgive? As many as seven times?' Jesus gives an answer that it is not seven times, but many times more than that. However, he immediately qualifies this with the parable of the unforgiving servant, which seems to have nothing to do with the focus in Peter's question, 'how many times.' Also, Peter's question involves only two people, himself and another member of his community. Yet Jesus' parable brings in many people – a lord, his servant whom the lord forgives, a fellow servant whom the forgiven servant refuses to forgive, and a group of fellow servants, who are distressed about what has happened and want to see justice done. Hence, although this parable appears to be about forgiveness, it is also about the question of justice in the context of seeking forgiveness or reconciliation.

Unlike in other contexts of forgiveness with justice, where the offender is powerful and the victim is powerless, here the one who seeks forgiveness is actually in a lowly position, and the one who grants forgiveness is in a higher position. The connection with justice is clearly that if we want to receive forgiveness, then we need to give it to others.

There are at least three sets of people with a sense of justice (or injustice) in the context of forgiveness: the unforgiving servant; the lord who forgives the servant but retracts his pardon later when the latter could not forgive his fellow servant; and the other servants who are displeased with the unforgiving servant for his actions towards his fellow servant.

The injustice of the forgiven servant

What the forgiven servant does is unjust because he needed forgiveness for a large debt, he sought it and he received it. Now he needs to forgive his fellow servant a much smaller debt, but refuses to do so. His attitude is not helpful. He completely fails to relate to his fellow servant because he fails to remember how his master has treated him. He has been forgiven something like 70 times but is not willing to forgive just once. He uses one measure for himself and a completely different one for his fellow servant, even though they are in the same difficult circumstances. He subverts the golden rule: 'Do to others as you would have them do to you' (Luke 6.31). Jesus challenges such a mindset through this parable and teaches us that, in the context of reconciliation and building relationships, one needs to do to others how one wants to be treated by others. This is really radical and essential: forgiveness happens to be the example here, but it may be replaced by any number of things.

The parable also talks about the changing nature of the victim and the oppressor, which is an important consideration in our reconciliation ministry today. A victim in one context can be an oppressor in another at the same time. Even as the servant is forgiven, he refuses to forgive his fellow servant. There is no strict binary division here – the story shows that the victim in one context is the oppressor in another. We can easily see how yesterday's victim can be today's oppressor or yesterday's oppressor today's victim – it is very fluid.

Indeed, victimhood is a concept that is becoming much debated today. While there are real and actual victims of injustice and exploitation, nowadays there is a tendency for powerful people, powerful communities and even powerful nations to see themselves as victims, irrespective of their place in society or the world. Considering themselves superior to real victims, one of their main reasons for playing the victim card is that it actually enables them to continue oppressing those who are suffering. It is worth pondering our own conduct here. Few of us avoid behaving this way at times in our personal lives. But the problem with so many of us pushing our case for victimhood is that we tend not to bother about real victims at all, and this is hugely detrimental to our relationships with one another and the ministry of reconciliation.

The lord's sense of justice

Second, the lord's sense of justice is important. Initially, out of compassion, he forgives all the debts of his servant, but for his forgiveness to be effective, the forgiven servant needs to forgive his fellow servant. The lord is not concerned only with the relationship between him and the forgiven servant; he does not see his servant being at peace with him as adequate. Rather the lord-servant relationship is affected by how the forgiven servant relates with others. The lord does not say, what matters is the relationship between you and me, and you can treat other people as you like, as far as I'm concerned. It is not the kind of set up we have in political relationships: be good to me and I don't mind what you do to others. Dictatorships in many countries in the world have been founded upon such attitudes, which has led to the suffering of millions of people. Yet the lord in this parable has a sense of justice, his forgiveness is withdrawn because the forgiven servant fails to act justly.

The fellow servants and their act of justice

Third, significant (though they may appear insignificant) are the fellow servants who are watching what is going on. They somehow know that the lord has forgiven the servant's debts. They have also witnessed the forgiven servant refusing to forgive his fellow servant. They are unable to be at peace because they know that what is happening here is not justice. They express their sense of injustice in at least in two ways. First, they become unhappy and feel sad about what the servant does. They are not neutral, but show solidarity with the servant against the unforgiving servant. Second, they do not leave the matter there, but take it to the lord. They are not silent, they believe they have a responsibility to act. Perhaps, if they had said nothing, what the forgiven servant did to his fellow servant would not have been brought to the notice of the lord at all. However, they feel justice has not been served, and even though there is no benefit for them, they act in response.

Peter asks a question about how many times he should forgive, but Jesus offers an example of someone who was forgiven but refuses to forgive. The primary point is that everyone who is in a position to forgive others is always in the need of forgiveness too – both from God and from our fellow human beings against whom we commit mistakes. It is important to look at the roles here. Unlike the other contexts, where the victim's forgiveness of the offender is important for reconciliation, and the offender needs to do justice to make the reconciliation process effective, here the offender is one who seeks forgiveness as a victim, but refuses to give it to his own victim, and thus does not act justly in the context of reconciliation.

Questions for reflection

1 When we are unwilling to forgive someone we have wronged, although we need forgiveness from them and are forgiven regularly by God and others, why might this be?
2 Why do you think the servant didn't forgive his fellow servant in spite of being forgiven himself? What factors do you think might have been at play here?
3 In what way does the lord in the parable act justly by wanting his servant to forgive his fellow servant as he has forgiven him?

40 Reconciliation only with God?

Key texts: Psalm 51 and 2 Samuel 12–13
David's confession of sins

The influence of Psalm 51 on our spiritual life and formation is enormous, and there is a significant place for it in our worship and liturgy. David's confession to God, as he seeks forgiveness and reconciliation after sinning against God (and others!), is a foundational prayer for our own confession of sin and reconciliation with God.

A remarkable thing about David's prayer is that it helps us (as it helped him) to go through the process of overcoming our guilt and seeking forgiveness for our sins. It reflects the humility needed for this. When the prophet Nathan confronts David, David immediately accepts that he has sinned against God and humbles himself. That he is a king does not matter one jot. He does not defend his actions or exalt himself before God, and his humility is accepted by God. In his prayer, David expresses his need for God's mercy and grace in living with his sin and the guilt that comes from it. He *relies* on God's abundant mercy and grace (verse 1). Admitting that he knows his transgressions is an important realization for David (verse 3a); he understands that God is justified in sentencing and is blameless in passing judgement (verse 4b). David is submitting himself and waiting for God to teach him wisdom (verse 6).

Yet, in the context of what David has done and all that has happened, his prayer is incomplete. David gives the impression that sin, and thus reconciliation, is primarily a matter between us and God. Is this the case? Those David has sinned against are entirely absent from his prayer. Not only does he fail to speak about making reparation to his victims, we don't see him remembering them once. Most of the time, do we not sin against God *because* we sin against our fellow human beings? How can reconciliation only with God then be sufficient? Let us explore this further.

First, David's prayer for forgiveness and reconciliation, even though spoken in humility, is all about him. The use of 'I' and 'me' could be evidence of the realization he has lately come to, but surely this involves other people as well. David uses the first person singular 36 times in the Psalm. It is about what he has done, certainly, but mainly about *what he wants for himself.* He speaks of what he feels, what he needs and what he wants. In verse 3, he says that 'my sin is ever before me.' Although it appears that he acknowledges his troublesome sinful nature, his unhappiness is actually about his sin continuously haunting him. In other words, he is concerned about what his sin is doing to *him.* He talks about *his* cleanliness (verses 1–3, 7, 9–10). He prays for *his* joy and gladness and readiness to sing praises (verses 8, 12, 14, 15). His victims have no place in his prayer at all!

Second, David does mention other people in his prayer, although they are not those affected by his transgressions. In verse 5, he blames his mother for giving birth to him in sin. He says, 'Indeed, I was born guilty, a sinner when my mother conceived me.' It is indeed important to affirm the root of our sinful nature, which we believe stems from the Garden of Eden, but this does not absolve one of one's own sin. Our mothers giving birth to us in sin cannot become our excuse for all the evil we do. It is important to remember what God says through Moses and confirms later during the prophets' time: 'A child shall not suffer for the iniquity of a parent, nor a parent suffer for the iniquity of a child (Ezekiel 18.20). David also talks about other sinners in verse 13. He seeks forgiveness and reconciliation with God so that he can preach God's ways to them. Yet in this rush to educate others, there is still no mention of those David has harmed. He is willing to teach sinners, but does he have the willingness in his heart to listen to his victims?

Third, perhaps the most difficult part of this prayer is when David says that he has sinned against God and God alone:

> Against you, you alone, have I sinned,
>   and done what is evil in your sight,
> so that you are justified in your sentence
>   and blameless when you pass judgment.   (verse 4)

David may have a point here: ultimately God's forgiveness is important. However, David's prayer neglects the fact that his sin has damaged the lives of several people, in addition to displeasing God. In 2 Samuel 12.13, David says to the prophet Nathan, 'I have sinned against the Lord.' It is true that only God can put away the sin in the end, but one cannot simply walk away as if one's sin has not affected others: David has definitely sinned against Bathsheba, Uriah, the people who trusted him, and those he used to get rid of Uriah and others.

David's affirmation suggests that when we sin, we feel happy only when we are forgiven by God. Of course, there may be sins in our individual lives about which it is only possible to ask forgiveness from God, but in our thoughts, planning and actions, we sin against one another. All our sins in some way involve other people, and so they affect our community or social life, even when we do not realize or want to acknowledge this.

It is often difficult for us to seek forgiveness from those we have wounded before we seek God's forgiveness. However, until and unless we reconcile with our victims, our reconciliation with God is not real, even if we think we have settled things. Jesus talks about this clearly in the Sermon in the Mount: 'So when you are offering your gift at the altar, if you remember that your brother or sister has something against you, leave your gift there before the altar and go; first be reconciled to your brother or sister, and then come and offer your gift' (Matthew 5.23–24).

Fourth, David is not at all concerned about the impact of his sins on his victims. In verse 11 he prays for his safety; in verse 17 he talks about a broken spirit, obviously referring to the situation he is in. Yet what about the spirits he himself has broken? What about his victims' lives? In his main accusation, the prophet Nathan begins by pointing out that David's killing of Uriah has led to the loss of a life, a woman to lose her husband, and David bearing responsibility for a child who is to die. In addition, David has been cunning in getting rid of Uriah on the battleground, wilfully allowing his own soldier – who was fighting a battle for his king – to die at the hands of his enemies. When responding to the prophet Nathan (in the story of the little ewe lamb that precedes Nathan's unvarnished telling of the truth), David says that the committer of sin should die, he should restore four times what he has taken, and this – importantly for David – because *he had no pity* (2 Samuel 12.5–6). Pity towards his victims, though, is completely lacking in David's prayer to God for forgiveness – he is unable to utter a single word for them.

Obviously, David did not sin only against God. He may have believed being forgiven by God was essential so that he could carry on with his life. When we pray to God seeking forgiveness for our own sins against others, we may do so with the same purpose, but do we not often think that asking for forgiveness from God and reconciling with God is *easier* than reconciling with the people who have been offended and affected by our actions? What the Apostle John tells us in his first epistle about loving God is also relevant to reconciling with God. He says: 'Those who say, "I love God," and hate their brothers or sisters, are liars; for those who do not love a brother or sister whom they have seen, cannot love God whom they have not seen' (1 John 4.20). John's words also have implications for seeking forgiveness and reconciliation with others. If we are not willing to ask forgiveness from someone whom we have seen and against whom we have sinned, how can we ask it of the unseen God?

David's prayer is indeed an excellent prayer for the forgiveness of his sins. However, from his victims' point of view, it has many limitations, because he prays as if the damage he has wrought is only between him and God. David wasn't offered a victim impact statement from Bathsheba or Uriah. If he had been, it would have been difficult for him to pray this way. At the very least, he would have had to make some additions!

No doubt, Psalm 51 is an important prayer in our Christian life, liturgy and worship and valuable for personal understanding and transformation, but we need to resist making our confession very individualistic. The Psalm completely excludes those we have hurt, what they feel, how they have been impacted by our sins and what should be done for them. Reconciliation with God – although ultimately necessary and important – cannot be a substitute for becoming reconciled with others. It cannot become an escape route for us, a way of bypassing our responsibilities to those we have sinned against. Yes, reconciling with God is the primary thing, but is it dangerous if one talks about reconciling *only* with God. The Bible has a clear message: relationship with God does not matter at all if relationship is not maintained with our fellow human beings.

In the history of the Church, sin and reconciliation has predominantly been seen from the perspective of the offender, who needs to confess and be forgiven by God. What would happen if we tried to understand sin from the perspective of those offended and to reconcile with this understanding? Andrew Sung Park and Susan L. Nelson in the introduction to their challenging book, *The Other Side of Sin: Woundedness from the Perspective of the Sinned Against* (2001), remark:

> For the past two thousand years, we have inadequately treated the victims of sin by neglecting to formulate doctrines for them while they walked through the valley of the shadow of death. Based on

the doctrine of sin, the Church has developed a map of the salvific doctrines for sinners or offenders: the doctrines of regeneration, justification by faith, sanctification by faith, and glorification or Christian perfection. It is time for the Church to think about a salvific path for the sinned-against. To do so, we need to understand the pain of the wounded, listening to their agonies and studying biblical, historical, and theological messages for their salvation. *The other side of sin* is . . . to start a new journey of faith for the sinned-against.

The Church has been facilitating sinners' reconciliation with God because of God's concern for sinners. God's abundant mercies are available to all of us, and we should never doubt God's everlasting love, unfailing kindness and readiness to forgive us when we repent of our sins. To be fully faithful to the ministry of reconciliation that Jesus has entrusted upon us, however, it is time to look at forgiveness, justice and reconciliation from the perspective of those who are being sinned against, because God's concern for victims remains unambiguous. We need to focus on what offenders need to do for victims, even as they seek forgiveness from and reconciliation with God.

As I am completing the studies for this Lent book, there is news that the martyred Archbishop Oscar Romero's canonization in the Church, which was long due, has just taken place. Fr. Dean Brackley, who worked towards this, said a few years ago about Romero's work:

> The Church will only be the bearer of credible hope for humanity if it stands with the poor, with all who are *victims* of sin, injustice and violence. If we walk with them, as Romero did, we will embody the good news that the world so longs for.

The Church's ministry of reconciliation is indeed about walking with victims, even as we invite offenders to reconcile and to act justly. In so doing we *embody the good news that the world so longs for*.

Questions for reflection

1 Confessing our sins to God alone is not sufficient. Why do we find it so difficult to reconcile with those we have sinned against?
2 In what ways can we involve our victims in our confession and growth in faith and understanding?
3 We are not reconciled with God until we are reconciled with those we have offended and offer them justice. How does this impact our reconciliation ministry?